"Toxic relationships can change the trajectory of a p
I Let You Go? addresses destructive attachments wit
ing the person who makes unworthy choices as 'damaged.' Each chapter
gives the reader insight, direction, and support. This is an important book
for anyone who dates or lives with manipulative or malevolent partners, or
has someone they care about who continually enters toxic relationships."

> —**Pepper Schwartz, PhD**, emeritus professor at the University
> of Washington, and on-air relationship expert for *Married at
> First Sight*

"In this masterful guide for anyone suffering through destructive relationship patterns, Michelle and Kelly Skeen make the reader feel supported,
validated, and not alone. You'll be guided through the process of identifying your attachment style, temperament, and core beliefs—and you'll learn
how to distinguish 'intensity' from 'intimacy.' In the end, you'll come away
with a better understanding of yourself, the types of partners you're
attracted to, and how to change."

> —**Jonice Webb, PhD**, internationally best-selling author of
> *Running on Empty* and *Running on Empty No More*

"The Skeens have done a remarkable job of intertwining and integrating
the most crucial concepts that affect intimate relationships. By incorporating interesting and deeply human personal stories into the presentation,
they create a perfect marriage between theory and implementation.
Readers will be able to internalize and personalize interrelationship skills
that will ensure more successful relationships in their futures, no matter
how they may have failed in the past."

> —**Randi Gunther, PhD**, clinical psychologist in Southern
> California; author of *Relationship Saboteurs* and *Heroic Love*;
> and author of more than 250 articles on *Psychology Today*

"This is an important book to figure out core beliefs, attachment style, and why intimacy can be triggering. The authors show readers how to set boundaries and stay true to their own values, giving clear direction and advice for moving forward, freeing themselves from trauma-bonded relationships. Everyone in our society today who has been touched by trauma should read this book."

—**Tammy Nelson, PhD**, sex and relationship therapist;
TEDx speaker; host of the podcast, *The Trouble with Sex*;
and author of six books, including *Open Monogamy*

"The relationship trauma bond (RTB)—formed from traumatic and insecure attachments to childhood caregivers—drives us to seek and cling to romantic partners who treat us the same way; who serially abandon and hurt us, but also make us feel safe because they are familiar and help us reenact the original trauma bond. The trauma bond is a trap, and *Why Can't I Let You Go?* is the key to escape. This wise and deeply understanding book can liberate you from negative, trauma-based beliefs that make you expect hurt and abandonment, and then attach to the very people whose MO is to hurt, criticize, and reject. Readers will learn how to recognize these people, let go of the addictive and damaging 'chemistry' inherent in the trauma bond, and use the book's powerful, evidence-based tools from acceptance and commitment therapy (ACT) to find true love."

—**Matthew McKay, PhD**, coauthor of *Acceptance
and Commitment Therapy for Interpersonal Problems,
Couple Skills,* and *Self-Esteem*

"*Why Can't I Let You Go?* is a compassionate guide to a deeper understanding of your emotional makeup and what drives your inclinations when it comes to partner selection. Michelle Skeen has done it again! In this thoughtfully written book, she provides her readers with effective strategies and solutions for getting unstuck from self-defeating patterns, trauma bonds, and toxic partners; moving you toward healthy and loving relationships."

—**Wendy Behary, LCSW**, author of *Disarming the Narcissist*

"Breaking free from unhealthy relationships can create confusion and fear. Michelle and Kelly, an insightful mother–daughter duo, offer us a master class in how to understand our emotions and develop a deep respect for ourselves. They offer us practical skills to help solve real-world relationship problems. *Why Can't I Let You Go?* is a compassionate and essential guide for anyone looking for wisdom, encouragement, and support to make powerful life changes."

—**Rebecca E. Williams, PhD**, psychologist, wellness expert, and author of *Simple Ways to Unwind without Alcohol*

"*Why Can't I Let You Go?* is an excellent resource for anyone who wonders why they stay trapped in the same old unsatisfying relationships. Michelle and Kelly Skeen are an outstanding duo."

—**Shawn T. Smith**, author of *The User's Guide to the Human Mind*

"*Why Can't I Let You Go?* is a go-to guide for people who want to end their toxic relationships and finally enjoy healthy connections. It provides clear explanations and effective exercises to help readers develop self-awareness related to replaying unhealthy childhood relationships. It also guides readers in developing the self-compassion needed for healing, and teaches them tools for building healthy attachments."

—**Leslie Becker-Phelps, PhD**, author of *Insecure in Love* and
Bouncing Back from Rejection

"*Why Can't I Let You Go?* is a compassionately crafted, thought-provoking, and transformative self-help book that assists readers in breaking free from their relationship trauma bond. The authors use an evidence-informed approach to increase self-awareness and promote a deeper understanding of unhealthy relationship patterns. Readers will benefit by exploring the 'why' behind their relationship behaviors. Most importantly, readers will learn the necessary tools to build healthy relationships to empower change and liberate them from their past."

—**Raychelle Cassada Lohmann, PhD**, clinician, educator,
speaker, and author of *The Anger Workbook for Teens*

"Michelle Skeen and Kelly Skeen have written a much-needed book. Their incorporation of attachment theory and core beliefs into the toxic relationship framework is essential reading."

—**Stephanie Moulton Sarkis, PhD**, psychotherapist, and author
of *Gaslighting* and *Healing from Toxic Relationships*

Why can't I let you go?

**Break Free from Trauma Bonds,
End Toxic Relationships, and
Develop Healthy Attachments**

MICHELLE SKEEN, PSYD | KELLY SKEEN

New Harbinger Publications, Inc.

Publisher's Note

This publication is designed to provide accurate and authoritative information in regard to the subject matter covered. It is sold with the understanding that the publisher is not engaged in rendering psychological, financial, legal, or other professional services. If expert assistance or counseling is needed, the services of a competent professional should be sought.

NEW HARBINGER PUBLICATIONS is a registered trademark of New Harbinger Publications, Inc.

New Harbinger Publications is an employee-owned company.

The attachment style assessment in chapter 1 is adapted from Simpson, J., W. S. Rholes, and D. Phillips. 1996. "Conflict in Close Relationships: An Attachment Perspective." Journal of Personality and Social Psychology, 71, 899–914. Copyright © 1996 by the American Psychological Association. Adapted with permission.

Cover design by Amy Shoup

Acquired by Elizabeth Hollis Hansen

Edited by Gretel Hakanson

Library of Congress Cataloging-in-Publication Data on file

Printed in the United States of America

26   25   24

10   9   8   7   6   5   4   3   2   1   First Printing

For Matt McKay

Contents

Introduction

It started with an instant emotional, and often, sexual intensity. Early on, there was an irresistible urge to merge. You felt like you'd known this person for longer than you had—they felt familiar. You even believed you'd found "the one." Then, they pulled away. They started to devalue you, find fault with you, blame you for problems between the two of you. They'd run hot and cold—they couldn't get enough of you, and then they'd had enough of you. When you reached a point where you didn't think you could take the abuse anymore, you made a move to end the relationship. They pulled you back in with promises and apologies. And the cycle began again. You found it difficult or impossible to end the relationship because you felt a deep emotional attachment that made it painful for you to imagine your life without them. This is a relationship trauma bond (RTB).

Here are a few questions to help you determine if you are in an RTB:

- Do you find yourself attracted to a "type"?

- Do you feel a connection that is familiar?

- Do you make excuses for their behavior toward you?

- Do you find yourself not speaking up due to a fear of rejection?

- Do you find yourself enduring hurtful behavior?

- Do you feel anxious or out of sorts when you're not with them?

- Do you find it difficult or impossible to end the relationship?

- Do you worry about losing them?

- When the relationship ends, do you find it challenging to move on? Or do you find yourself going back to give it another try?

If you answered yes to several of these questions, you might be engaged in an RTB.

What Is a Relationship Trauma Bond?

Our attachments to significant people in our lives begin at birth. They are influenced by our temperament as children, the caregivers we have, and the interaction between the two. In general, a healthy attachment results in a sense of security in relationships—an experience of being valued and feeling positive about relationships. An unhealthy attachment results in feelings associated with abandonment, defectiveness, mistrust, and anxiety. These early relationships form our beliefs about ourselves, others, and the world around us. Unhealthy foundational relationships—those formed in childhood—will likely distort our view of our adult relationships and result in unhealthy relationship dynamics.

When we're children, we have very little, if any, control over our relationships. Affecting change in our early relationships is impossible. In childhood, we depend on the person or people who helped form our core beliefs. When we mature into adulthood, we gain a sense of power over ourselves and our choices. On a conscious or unconscious level, we want to take control of our relationships. This desire often drives us to the same type of person(s) who caused our RTB.

In these adult relationships, you also feel like you need this person for safety and survival. You experience connection because these people feel familiar—like you've known them for longer than you have. You experience heightened arousal, which can feel like the "butterflies" that are a bodily sensation associated with attraction. Each of these relationships is a cycle in the reenactment of the trauma you experienced as a child. You were consciously or unconsciously drawn to the same type of person, believing that this is what you deserve or that this time, it will be different and they will finally see your worth and love you as you deserve and yearn to be loved.

You may already be aware of your drive to seek out similar types of people or to be drawn to situations that are reminiscent of the conditions of your original trauma. Or you may be starting to realize that you have been unconsciously seeking partners or creating experiences that are keeping you stuck in the patterns associated with the trauma from your developmental years. Either way, you are re-exposing yourself to people and environments that are keeping your original trauma activated. You are stuck in reliving RTBs.

As you explore RTBs throughout this book, you may experience negative emotions that are challenging to deal with. If you find yourself struggling, take care and consider speaking to a professional to help you process your experience. This book is just one part of your path to healing.

Exploring Your RTBs

Before we begin, consider why you picked up this book. Is there a particular relationship experience that brought you here? As you move forward, what are you hoping to learn about yourself? Let's set the stage for the work to come. Throughout the book, you'll use a journal to reflect on your experiences and develop the tools you need to break free from trauma bonds, end toxic relationships, and develop healthy attachments. You'll see questions for reflection within the text and more formal exercises. The exercises are designed to help you apply the frameworks and practice the skills, while the reflection questions are meant to provide you with the option of reflecting further on your experience, whether it's at the same time as you complete the exercises or a later time when you are revisiting the book. This is a good place to start. Respond to the questions above in your journal.

Let's take a look at what Casey wrote: "My most recent relationship made me realize that I struggle to develop healthy attachments. I want to understand the reason why it's hard for me and how I can best move forward. Rationally, I know I'm deserving of real love and that when I'm ready and I've done the work, the right person will come into my life. So, when I met my most recent ex I felt, almost immediately, like I'd known them for years. We slept together quickly because it just felt right—I had a feeling they were 'the one.' All the bad relationships and disappointments in my past suddenly made sense because it felt like I was about to get my reward for putting up with all of it. Things were great for a month or two— at least I thought so. Then, I began to feel a shift with them, but it was subtle at first. They started canceling our plans to hang out and taking longer to respond to my calls and texts. I didn't know if this change was in my head or not. Was this normal, after such a hot start? When I look back at it now, while it felt like a relationship to me, we hadn't actually had a conversation about exclusivity. We hadn't agreed on expectations, and so maybe I had a much different idea of what we had together than they did. The lack of information about how they felt about me was starting to make me feel panicked. They continued to pull away and eventually ended our time together pretty callously. I'm still confused about how the relationship felt so right to me at the outset but how my judgment had been so wrong. It ended the same way so many of my relationships in the past have ended! I realized that I'm drawn to people who disappear on me. It leaves me feeling that something is wrong with me. I want to understand why I keep getting left."

Can you relate to Casey's experience? Or maybe you are stuck in a relationship trauma bond or a series of RTBs. If so, the following situation might resonate with you.

Here's what Kai had to say about his RTB: "I've been in a four-year relationship with someone I'm very comfortable with—I mean comfortable in the sense that they're familiar to me. Growing up, I never received any positive reinforcement, encouraging words, or expressions of love. Even in my earliest memories I don't recall my parents ever telling me they loved me. Maybe that's what tough love looks like. I did receive support and encouragement from some of my friends, teachers, and bosses, but it wasn't a substitute for what was lacking in my family.

"Fast-forward, and here I am living with someone who treats me exactly like my parents did. Over the years, I've dated people who were complimentary of me and expressed positive reassuring feelings toward me, but I rejected them. Probably because it was unfamiliar to me, and maybe I didn't think I deserved it. But I'm starting to feel like I deserve more than what I'm getting. And the negativity has taken a toll on me. I think I'm in a relationship trauma bond, I feel stuck, and I need help getting out."

Whether you are in a toxic cycle of dating, like Casey, or you are stuck in an RTB, like Kai, this book is for you.

About This Book

Understanding yourself and your deeply held and often unconscious beliefs is the first step toward liberating yourself from toxic relationships. Chapter 1 will provide you with detailed explanations about attachment styles as well as an assessment to determine your attachment style. You'll get insight into the childhood experiences that created the RTB and laid the foundation for toxic relationships in adulthood. This will provide some context for the toxic relationship trap you find yourself stuck in. With the guidance of a nine-trait assessment, you'll also gain a greater understanding about your temperament. This is another foundational component of your interpersonal dynamics. You'll start to realize how much was out of your control during your formative years. This realization will allow you to let go of the self-doubt and shame that you've likely been carrying with you.

In chapter 2, you'll gain a new understanding of yourself through the lens of your core beliefs. You will complete self-assessments on the seven core beliefs that are most linked to RTBs. The core beliefs that laid the foundation for toxic relationships include abandonment, emotional deprivation, defectiveness, mistrust or abuse, dependence, subjugation, and failure. These core beliefs are illustrated in chapter 2 and throughout the book with stories. It's likely that you will relate to some of the stories; they'll give you confidence in knowing that you're not alone in what you're struggling with. At the end of chapter 2, you will have a greater understanding of what has been driving your relationship choices. You will also have increased self-compassion for the child in you who endured the interpersonal experiences that formed your core beliefs.

Chapter 3 will help you link your core beliefs with your behaviors and relationship choices. Through the process of identifying your behaviors, you'll begin to understand why they are causing you additional pain. These first three chapters are an examination of your past that can trigger emotional distress. But it's important to look at your past so you can understand it and leave behind the beliefs and behaviors that no longer serve you. This is a critical step to moving forward on your path toward the healthy life and love that you deserve.

Chapter 4 will revisit the unhelpful coping behaviors that you identified in chapter 3 and help you recognize the familiar "types" of people you find yourself attracted to as a result. You'll gain a better understanding of why you are drawn to relationship dynamics that are similar to those you experienced in childhood and adolescence. These types of people include the abandoner, the abuser, the controller, the critic, the depriver, and the devastator. We'll bring awareness to the manipulative strategies these types of people can use, how they target your vulnerabilities, and why the dynamic is keeping both of you stuck in an RTB.

Chapter 5 addresses a very important aspect of the RTB: the intensity. In this chapter, you'll gain a deeper understanding of the addictive qualities inherent in an RTB. High arousal and high risk are often mistaken for great "chemistry" and intimacy. The reality is that those intense feelings are often predictors of high drama, conflict, and betrayal coupled with passionate reconciliations. An RTB is intense, addictive, and unhealthy. This is a stark contrast to the qualities inherent in healthy intimacy: trust, mutual respect, and safety. Understanding the difference between the two will provide you with the knowledge you need to assist you in making healthy choices.

In chapter 6, you'll identify your values, including what you specifically value in a relationship, and compare those values to what you have in your current or recent relationship. Once you see the "gap" between the two, you will learn and apply cognitive and behavioral tools that will help you narrow, and ultimately, close the gap. It is a powerful experience to see the difference between where you are and where you want to be. It's even more powerful when you narrow and, ultimately, close the gap.

Healthy communication skills are covered in chapter 7. You'll identify the obstacles to healthy communication, and you'll be introduced to communication skills that will help you end the cycle of toxic communication.

Chapter 8 highlights the importance and power of mindfulness for staying present in the moment. A mindfulness practice will help you end the unhelpful automatic behaviors that result from situations that trigger you and dynamics that have you stuck in RTBs and toxic relationships.

Chapter 9 will provide you with tools to help you face the pain of loss that comes with liberating yourself from toxic relationships. You'll be guided through an acceptance and commitment therapy-based approach to processing the grief as well as the yearning that accompanies the end of a relationship, including an RTB.

In chapter 10, you'll learn strategies for identifying potential partners as well as tips and tools to guide you through the early stages of dating, when most people can get tripped up by triggers and traps.

In the final chapter, we provide you with a map for staying on the path to creating and living the life that you deserve.

This process will not be easy, but in time you will realize that it's easier and less painful than the heartache, hurt, and self-doubt you've been enduring for years. With increased knowledge and self-compassion, you'll embrace the belief that you deserve healthy, loving relationships and a value-driven life.

You won't be doing this alone. Let's get started on your new path together.

CHAPTER 1

Understanding Your Attachment Style and Temperament

An environment that provides a child with safety, security, and love will almost certainly create a secure attachment between the child and their caregiver and, eventually, others in the child's life. Unfortunately, research suggests that approximately 50 percent of children don't develop a secure attachment. If you are reading this book, it's likely that you have a different attachment style, through no fault of your own. Your childhood experiences create a narrative that resonates throughout your life.

This chapter focuses on temperament and attachment styles, which—along with core beliefs (the topic of chapter 2)—will lay the foundation for understanding yourself, your toxic relationships, your trauma bonds, and your unhealthy attachments. While you may already be aware of your attachment style, we want to encourage you to read this chapter and complete the assessment. You might also have a sense of your temperament, but often these parts of ourselves are operating outside of awareness. With this knowledge, you will learn the tools that will help you detach and make choices that are aligned with your values and what you deserve.

Attachment Styles

There are three primary attachment styles: secure, anxious, and avoidant. A person with a secure attachment would find it relatively easy to get close to others. They are comfortable depending upon others and having others depend upon them. And they don't tend to worry about being abandoned or someone getting too close to them.

If you have an anxious attachment style, you find that others are reluctant to get as close as you would like. You worry that your partner doesn't really love you or won't want to stay with you. Your desire to merge completely with another person often scares people away.

You have an avoidant attachment style if you are somewhat uncomfortable being close to others. You find it difficult to trust them completely and therefore struggle to allow yourself to depend upon them. It makes you nervous when someone gets too close. And you are uncomfortable with too much intimacy.

You might already have a sense of your attachment style from these descriptions, but the following statements from the Adult Attachment Questionnaire (AAQ), adapted from Simpson, Rholes, and Phillips (1996), will provide more clarity about your level of anxiety, dependency, and closeness.

Using the scale below, place a number between 1 and 5 next to each statement.

1———————— 2 ———————— 3 ———————— 4 ———————— 5

Not at all   Very
characteristic   characteristic
of me   of me

1. I find it relatively easy to get close to people. _____

2. I find it difficult to allow myself to depend on others. _____

3. I often worry that other people don't really love me. _____

4. I find that others are reluctant to get as close as I would like. _____

5. I am comfortable depending on others. _____

6. I don't worry about people getting too close to me. _____

7. I find that people are never there when you need them. _____

8. I am somewhat uncomfortable being close to others. _____

9. I often worry that other people won't want to stay with me. _____

10. When I show my feelings for others, I'm afraid they will not feel the same about me. _____

11. I often wonder whether other people really care about me. _____

12. I am comfortable developing close relationships with others. _____

13. I am uncomfortable when anyone gets too emotionally close to me. _____

14. I know that people will be there when I need them. _____

15. I want to get close to people, but I worry about being hurt. _____

16. I find it difficult to trust others completely. _____

17. People often want me to be emotionally closer than I feel comfortable being. _____

18. I am not sure that I can always depend on people to be there when I need them. _____

Let's look at the anxious attachment style.

You have an *anxious attachment style* if you marked 3, 4, 9, 10, 11, and 15 on the higher (3 to 5) end of the scale.

Meet Camila. She is twenty-eight years old, and she was born in the United States after her parents immigrated from the Dominican Republic. Her memories of her father are faint because he was deported when Camila was three years old. Her mother was loving toward her, but she worked three jobs to support them and send money to family members living in the DR. They had a tight-knit and supportive community of other DR immigrants near their home in Newark. The parents and extended family members shared childcare duties outside of the time the children spent in school. However, the caregiver was often the oldest child in the group. When her mother was with Camila, she was loving and attentive, which was soothing to her. But it wasn't enough. Camila felt anxious when she wasn't with her mother. Camila needed more emotional support, physical affection, and comfort than her mom was able to give.

Camila scored high on statement 3 (*I often worry that people don't really love me*), statement 9 (*I often worry that other people won't want to stay with me*), and statement 11 (*I often wonder whether other people really care about me*). High scores on these statements indicate that Camila has an anxious attachment style. In future chapters, we will look at how her attachment style interacts with her core beliefs and her temperament to create and reinforce relationship trauma bonds (RTBs).

Here is the scoring for the avoidant attachment style.

You have an *avoidant attachment style* if you marked 1, 5, 6, 12, and 14 on the lower (1 to 3) end of the scale and 2, 7, 8, 13, 16, 17, and 18 on the higher (3 to 5) end of the scale.

Now, let's meet someone with an avoidant attachment style. Here's Ian. His mother struggled with undiagnosed postpartum depression after he was born. Some days she couldn't get out of bed because she was easily overwhelmed. She was overcome with feelings of sadness, and this made it difficult for her to bond with her baby. Ian's father was present and loving toward Ian when he was not at work, but he was often overwhelmed by the task of taking care of his wife and his new baby. They were financially fortunate enough to hire a woman who looked after the house, Ian, and Ian's mother when his father was at work. Obviously, this was a painful experience for everyone in their family.

Ian's scores highlight his struggle. He scored low on statements 1 (*I find it relatively easy to get close to people*), 5 (*I am comfortable depending on others*), and 12 (*I am comfortable developing close relationships with others*). He scored high on statements 2 (*I find it difficult to allow myself to depend on others*), 8 (*I am somewhat uncomfortable being close to others*), 13 (*I am uncomfortable when anyone gets too emotionally close to me*), and 17 (*People often want me to be emotionally closer than I feel comfortable being*).

If your score indicates an anxious attachment style, you might be aware of the challenges of a relationship with someone who has an avoidant attachment. In fact, these pairings can often create RTBs. It's important to validate this experience while also noting that the avoidantly attached are not toxic as a group. As you'll see in the next two chapters, everyone is more complex than their attachment style. In other words, it is possible to be in a relationship with someone who has an avoidant attachment style without it creating an RTB.

Finally, let's look at the secure attachment style.

You have a *secure attachment style* if you are able to be close in relationships and depend upon others.

If you marked 1, 6, and 12 on the higher (3 to 5) end of the scale; and 8, 13, and 17 on the lower (1 to 3) end of the scale, you *are able to be close in relationships*.

If you marked statements 5 and 14 on the higher (3 to 5) end of the scale and statements 2, 7, 16, and 18 on the lower (1 to 3) end of the scale, you *are able to depend upon others*.

Meet Aryan. He grew up in Washington, DC, in a close-knit family of four with a brother who was four years older—and who passed away in an accident when they were both teens. Aryan and his brother were extremely close, and Aryan relied on him for guidance. He was a loving and dependable older brother, and they were raised by supportive and loving parents.

As expected, based on his profile, Aryan scored high on 1 (*I find it relatively easy to get close to people*), 6 (*I don't worry about people getting too *close to me*), and 12 (*I am comfortable developing close relationships with others*). This indicates that Aryan is able to be close in relationships. He also scored high on 5 (*I am comfortable depending on others*). Aryan has a secure attachment style, and he is able to be close in relationships and depend upon others.

You might be wondering why a securely attached person is being used as an example in a book about trauma bonds and toxic relationships. Good point! Attachment style is a predictor in relationship choices and dynamics, but it is not the only factor at play. In the next chapter, you will see how the presence of one or more core beliefs adds to the complexity of our relationships. You will learn more about Aryan and his relationship trauma bond in chapter 2.

Now that you've identified your attachment style, let's move on to an exercise that is designed to bring awareness to the experiences that contributed to your attachment. We'll share Camila's, Ian's, and Aryan's insights to help guide you through your exploration.

Attachment Style Statements

For each of the relevant statements from your results, write down any emotions, thoughts, and memories that come up for you.

Here are Camila's statements and related reactions:

3. I often worry that other people don't really love me. *I felt loved by my mother, but I never felt truly loved by my father. We spoke on the telephone often, and he sent cards for special occasions. But, as a little girl who didn't understand the complexity of deportation and immigration, I believed that if he really loved me, he would be with me and my mom.*

9. I often worry that other people won't want to stay with me. *This is also related to my dad. If my dad wouldn't stay with me, his only child, how can I expect anyone else to want to stay with me? And even though I know my mom was gone because she was working to support us, it still left a bit of a feeling that she didn't want to be with me.*

11. I often wonder whether other people really care about me. *As a young girl, I spent time outside of school with our close community of friends also from the DR. I was taken care of, but the other adults were struggling to make enough money, like my mom, so they didn't have the luxury of time with us kids. I attached quickly to the teachers at my school, but they changed every year, so there weren't any ongoing relationships. I guess that left me feeling like people were with me out of a sense of duty, not because they really cared about me.*

Here are Ian's statements and related reactions:

2. I find it difficult to allow myself to depend on others. *From the time I could remember, I didn't feel like I could depend upon anyone to be there for me all the time. My mom might have been physically present, but emotionally she had a "Do not disturb" sign up at all times. My dad loved me, but he was at work during the week and was pulled between me and my mom when he wasn't at work. I had the feeling that I shouldn't ask for much from either of them.*

8. I am somewhat uncomfortable being close to others. *The experience of being close to others is uncomfortable for me because it's unfamiliar. I didn't have any close friends growing up because I felt self-conscious about my home life.*

13. I am uncomfortable when anyone gets too emotionally close to me. *If being emotionally close is a skill, I never learned it. I never learned how to receive it or how to reciprocate it.*

17. People often want me to be emotionally closer than I feel comfortable being. *This is related to the statement above. I don't know how to be close.*

Here are Aryan's statements and related reactions:

1. I find it relatively easy to get close to people. *Growing up, I had a very close relationship with my older brother and my two moms. I felt safe with all of them.*

5. I am comfortable depending on others. *I was very dependent on my brother. He was four years older, and he was always there to guide me and protect me. With him gone, I don't feel certain that I'm capable of making decisions on my own. I tend to trust other people more than I trust myself. This has become a problem for me in my current relationship because I am dominated by a partner who has determined every aspect of our lives together. I can't express my opinions or feelings. Now, I realize that I'm very unhappy, but I feel trapped.*

6. I don't worry about people getting too close to me. *I was very close with my brother and my parents, and I never had an issue with people wanting to get close to me.*

12. I am comfortable developing close relationships with others. *Not only am I comfortable developing close relationships with others, but I feel like I need close relationships with others to feel secure.*

Did any of the emotions, thoughts, or memories from Camila, Ian, or Aryan resonate with your experiences? Take a moment to reflect on the statements from the questionnaire that felt most relevant to you and the accompanying emotions, thoughts, and memories. How do you feel about connecting your childhood experiences to your attachment style? Does it clarify some things for you, or do you feel nervous about or intimidated by the prospect of confronting what's emerging? All feelings are valid. Record your reflections in your journal if you feel inspired.

Camila's feelings about connecting her childhood experience to her attachment style were as follows: *It brought me back to the feelings I had as a child. I think as I got older, my narrative about my childhood and my family became detached from the emotions that I experienced as a child. I thought that my intense emotional responses to my girlfriend were related to her. Now I'm beginning to understand how much those experiences and emotions were related to my childhood.*

Here's what Ian had to say: *I hadn't realized how much I didn't learn about relationships when I was growing up. It's not that I don't want to get close* to others, depend upon others, or have others try to get close to me, but I don't know how to do it. I've never succeeded at it, so maybe I'm avoiding it so I don't feel like a failure.

Now, let's see what Aryan had to say: It reminded me of a wonderful time in my life when my family was together, and I felt loved and safe. It's filled with mixed emotions because I know I was so fortunate to grow up in that environment. Unfortunately, it felt like everything changed with the death of my brother.

Bringing awareness to your attachment style is one of many steps that you'll take on your path to greater self-knowledge. This information is meant to be useful in laying the foundation for understanding your RTBs. It's not meant to increase feelings of shame. Again, attachments are formed through interactions between an infant and their caregivers. As such, your attachment style is the result of factors that were out of your control. The relationship your caregivers had with you has influenced all your subsequent relationships, and it's had a powerful impact on your adult relationships. It created a script, a narrative for your subsequent relationships that is your default in relationships—but as an adult, you can control your script and you can change your narrative. Bringing your story into the light, seeing the way it's influenced your choices, and understanding why you are often drawn to toxic people are requirements for change; they're also what *allow* you to change.

Our attachment styles affect the way we handle relationship conflicts, feelings toward sex, and expectations in intimate relationships. But just because you've been relating to others in a way that is specific to your attachment style doesn't mean that you can't change. In fact, bringing your unconscious behaviors to awareness is progress on the path toward relating to others, and yourself, in ways that will get you closer to the love, safety, and security you desire and deserve (Simpson et al. 1996).

How are you feeling after taking this assessment? Do the results resonate with you? Did anything surprise you? Have you gotten a little more clarity about your narrative? Take the time you need to reflect on your results.

Temperament

Your attachment style is not the only element that influences your adult relationships. In addition to the environmental factors that contribute to the development of attachment styles, core beliefs and temperament play essential roles. A child's emotional temperament is important in understanding the emotional reactions to experiences that trigger core beliefs. Each child is born with a distinct personality—shy, energetic, sensitive, fearless, calm, anxious, passive, sociable, cheerful, aggressive—and these traits result in a variety of responses to their environment, including their relationships with others (BetterHelp Editorial Team 2023). A child's emotional temperament interacts with and reacts to painful childhood events, which create core beliefs. Over time, reactions to triggers become fixed, thereby reinforcing core beliefs. In chapter 3, we'll take a closer look at the unhelpful coping behaviors that result from the interplay of temperament, core beliefs, and attachment style.

Temperament can be understood as a personality type that you're born with or predisposed to. It plays a role in the way you experience your life as well as the way you react to others. In an effort to understand yourself better, including your reactions to triggering events, we have adapted Chess and Thomas's (1996) research on temperament. This addresses the "nature" piece of the complex interplay between "nature" and "nurture." Psychologists Alexander Thomas and Stella Chess developed a measure for nine traits (activity level, distractibility, response, rhythmicity and regularity, sensory sensitivity, response to new things, ability to adapt, attention span, and disposition) that make up one's temperament. As you read about the nine traits, make notes in your journal about where you fall on these measures. There are no right or wrong answers. This is designed to help you bring greater awareness to yourself and your experiences (Bidjerano 2011).

We've created a Likert scale of 1 to 5. After each trait, we'll share Ian's, Aryan's, and Camila's responses, so you will see how the three foundational components we're assessing in these first two chapters come together. At the end of this assessment, we'll provide a summary of all three.

1. Activity level

1 ——————— 2 ——————— 3 ——————— 4 ——————— 5

Low
energy

Energetic

Do you identify as being low energy, high energy, or somewhere in between? Write about your energy level in your journal.

- Camila scored a 5 on this scale. Here's what she wrote in her journal: *I have a high energy level.*

- Ian marked a 4 on this scale. Here's what he wrote: *As an adult, I have a fairly high energy level. But when I was growing up, I wasn't in an environment where I could fully express it.*

- Aryan gave himself a 3. Here's what he wrote: *I feel like I have average energy. I can rise to the occasion if something requires a lot of energy, but I'm also happy just taking it easy.*

2. Distractibility

1 ——————— 2 ——————— 3 ——————— 4 ——————— 5

Easily
distracted

Able to
maintain
focus

Are you easily distracted even when it's something you're interested in, or are you able to maintain focus even with a boring task, or do you fall somewhere in between? Write about it in your journal.

- Camila is a 4 on this trait. Here's what she wrote: *I can be highly focused. It's a great trait in my career, but it tends to be a problem in my relationships.*

- Ian is a 3 on the distractibility trait. He wrote: *I'm not easily distracted, but I don't have a strong ability to focus.*

- Aryan gave himself a 2. He wrote: *I have a difficult time staying focused. I am easily distracted.*

3. Response

1 ——————— 2 ——————— 3 ——————— 4 ——————— 5

Remain   Respond
calm   intensely

Are you able to remain calm when you are faced with an upsetting or triggering situation, or do you have trouble controlling your emotional response? Or do you fall somewhere in between? Write your response in your journal.

- Camila gave herself a 4. She wrote: *I respond intensely when I'm in a triggering situation. It's been a problem for me in my relationships.*

- Ian identifies as a 1. Here's what he wrote: *I'm able to remain calm when faced with an upsetting or triggering situation. I feel like I was conditioned to remain calm because my mom was incapable of handling an emotional response from me.*

- Aryan identifies as a 3. Here's what he wrote: *I feel like I have pretty normal responses to situations. If it's less personal, I can remain calm; if it's more personal, I can be more emotional.*

4. Rhythmicity and regularity

1 ——————— 2 ——————— 3 ——————— 4 ——————— 5

Unstructured
and no
routine

Structured
and routined

Do you require structure and a routine and find it upsetting when your structure or routine is changed? Or do you prefer your life to be unstructured? Or are you somewhere in between? Write about it in your journal.

- Camila identified as a 2. Here's her response: *I'm not very good with structure. It's challenging for me to stick to a routine.*

- Ian considers himself a 4 on this trait. He wrote: *My life was very structured when I was growing up because of the nature of my home environment.*

- Aryan is a 5. He wrote: *Structure and a routine are very important to me. I like my life to be predictable.*

5. Sensory sensitivity

1 ——————— 2 ——————— 3 ——————— 4 ——————— 5

Don't react
to changing
stimuli

React strongly
to changing
stimuli

Are you sensitive to change in stimuli in your environment, or are you unmoved by them? Write about your reaction to changing stimuli in your journal.

- Camila is a 3. She wrote: *I'm fine with changing stimuli. In fact, I tend to like it.*

- Ian identifies with a 3 on sensory sensitivity. Here is his response: *I feel like I have a normal reaction to stimuli in my environment.*

- Aryan scored this a 5. Here's what he wrote: *I react very strongly to changing stimuli in my environment. Similar to the previous statement,*

I like my life to be predictable, and that includes disliking/avoiding changing stimuli in my environment.

6. Response to new things

1———————2———————3———————4———————5

Withdraw when
faced with
a problem

Address the
problem
head-on

When you are facing a challenging situation, do you have a tendency to withdraw, or do you address the problem head-on? Or are you somewhere in between? Write about your experience with your response to new things in your journal.

- Camila identified as a 4 on this scale. Here's what she wrote: *If I'm facing a challenge, I tend to address it head-on—I don't retreat.*

- Ian marked a 2 on this scale. He wrote: *I have more of a tendency to withdraw when faced with a problem or something new to deal with.*

- Aryan scored this statement with a 1. He wrote: *I am not good at facing challenging situations. I completely withdraw. It's something I want to work on.*

7. Ability to adapt

1———————2———————3———————4———————5

Difficulty
adapting to
new situations

Embrace
new situations

Changes are constantly happening in our lives. Do you have difficulty adapting to changes and new situations, or do you embrace changes and new situations? Write about your tendency in your journal. Pay particular attention to this if you are stuck in a trauma bond. If you have difficulty adapting to changes or new situations, this could be a contributing factor in keeping you stuck in an RTB.

- Camila scored a 4 on this trait. She wrote: *I don't have a problem adapting to new situations. In fact, I find myself drawn to them.*

- Ian identified as a 3 on this trait. Here's his journal entry: *I don't have difficulty adapting to new situations, but I'm also not particularly drawn to new situations. I do recognize that meeting new people is difficult for me. If that's considered a new situation, then I would mark myself a 2.*

- Aryan identifies as a 1. Here's what he wrote: *This is another tough one for me. I have difficulty adapting to new situations. I go to great lengths to avoid them.*

8. Attention span

1 —————— 2 ————— 3 ————— 4 ————— 5

Lose interest
quickly

Able to focus
for extended
periods of time

Do you lose interest in tasks and situations quickly? Or are you able to focus for extended periods of time? Record your experience in your journal.

- Camila gave herself a 4. She wrote: *I'm able to focus for extended periods of time if I need to.*

- Ian identifies as a 3 on this statement. He wrote: *I feel like I'm in the middle on this one. I don't lose interest quickly, but I'm not really great at focusing for extended periods of time.*

- Aryan gave himself a 3. Here's what he wrote: *I feel like I'm solidly in the middle on this one. I can focus for a while, and I might lose interest after an extended period of time, but not quickly.*

9. Disposition

1 —————— 2 —————— 3 —————— 4 —————— 5

More prone
to a sad
mood

More prone
to a happy
mood

Do you tend to be more prone to feeling down, depressed, or sad? Or are you more inclined to be in a happy or upbeat mood? You might think about how you feel when you wake up in the morning: Are you ready to greet the day, or do you experience feelings of dread? Or are you somewhere in between? Write about your disposition in your journal.

- Camila gave herself a 4. Here's what she wrote about her disposition: *I tend to wake up in the morning ready to take on the day. I'm generally a happy person. I can get down about things—especially relationships—but overall, I think I have a good outlook.*

- Ian scored a 2 on this trait. Here's what he wrote in his journal: *Growing up, I never had a smiling face greeting me in the morning. My mom was struggling with depression, so if I saw her, she was sad. Our housekeeper was a nice person, but she had a lot to deal with, and during the week, my dad had already left for work by the time I got up. I think I just got used to starting my day with a solemn outlook.*

- Aryan scored a 3. He wrote: *I'm solidly in the middle on this trait. But when I was younger, I would have given myself a 5. That had a lot to do with my brother.*

How do you feel after completing this assessment of your temperament? Did it bring awareness to parts of your personality that have been operating out of your awareness? If so, you're not alone. We rarely have the opportunity to do a deep dive into ourselves. Write about your experience in your journal.

Here is a summary of Camila's temperament self-assessment:

- *She is very energetic.*

- *She can be highly focused.*

- *She responds intensely when she gets triggered.*

- *She's not good with structure.*

- *She responds well to changing stimuli.*

- *She addresses challenges head-on.*

- *She adapts well to new situations.*

- *She can focus for extended periods of time.*

- *She is generally a happy person.*

Here is Camila's post-assessment reflection: *Wow! Looking at myself through this lens makes me recognize that I can be A LOT. I've heard it plenty of times, but somehow seeing it in this way brings a new perspective for me. This, coupled with my anxious attachment style, brings some clarity to my relationship experiences.*

Here is the summary of Ian's temperament self-assessment:

- *He has a fairly high energy level.*

- *He's not easily distracted.*

- *He can remain calm when he's faced with an upsetting situation.*

- *He is structured and routined.*

- *He has a normal reaction to changing stimuli in his environment.*

- *He tends to withdraw when faced with a problem.*

- *He doesn't have difficulty adapting to new situations, but he finds it challenging when meeting new people.*

- *He has an average attention span.*

- *His disposition tends to be more subdued.*

Ian wrote this about his post-assessment experience: *It was interesting to look at these different traits. Reflecting on my attachment style as well as my traits, I have a better understanding about why I might find it challenging to develop close relationships.*

Here is a summary of Aryan's temperament self-assessment:

- *He has an average energy level.*

- *He has a difficult time staying focused; he is easily distracted.*

- *He has normal responses to triggering situations.*

- *Structure and routine are very important to him.*

- *He reacts strongly to changing stimuli.*

- *He's not good at facing challenging situations.*

- *He has difficulty adapting to new situations.*

- *He's fine focusing for a while.*

- *He is neither sad or happy—he's solidly in the middle.*

Here's what Aryan wrote about his takeaway from the self-assessment: *This was an eye-opener for me. I feel like my responses to traits highlight the problems in my life right now. I'm not happy in my relationship, but I don't do anything to change it. I can see why: I like structure and routine, I react strongly to changing stimuli, I'm not good at facing challenging situations, and I have difficulty adapting to new situations. This is why I'm stuck.*

Moving Forward

This chapter is loaded with information designed to help you understand two of the complex components—attachment style and temperament—that make up your interpersonal narrative and likely leave you stuck in a pattern of relationship trauma bonding or toxic relationship dynamics. In the next chapter, you will take seven self-assessments to determine which of the core beliefs is operating outside of your awareness and negatively impacting the relationships with yourself, others, and the world around you. And you will hear more from Camila, Ian, and Aryan as they put all the foundational self-assessments together to get a clearer picture of themselves.

Let's keep going.

CHAPTER 2

The Core of the Relationship Trauma Bond

The goal with this book is to compassionately guide you along a path to a greater understanding of yourself and your relationships to others. To that end, we are focusing on three elements that deeply influence who you are: attachment style, temperament, and core beliefs. In the previous chapter, you brought awareness to your attachment style and nine traits that can be attributed to your temperament. In this chapter, you will identify the core beliefs that have been unconsciously driving your relationship and behavioral choices. We will be looking at the seven core beliefs that are linked to relationship trauma bonds (RTBs): abandonment, mistrust and abuse, emotional deprivation, defectiveness, dependence, failure, and subjugation.

What Are Core Beliefs?

According to Jeffrey Young (Young, Klosko, and Weishaar 2006), maladaptive schemas (we call them *core beliefs*) are created when early childhood needs—basic safety, connection with others, autonomy, self-esteem, and self-expression—aren't met. The core beliefs that result are problematic for people and their relationships. A core belief is essentially a belief about yourself and your relationship to the world. These beliefs form in part as a result of dysfunctional experiences in childhood. That includes our relationships with parents, caregivers, siblings, and peers. Repeated toxic messages—verbal and nonverbal—contribute to our core beliefs. Once a core belief is formed, it is extremely stable, and it becomes an enduring pattern of emotions, behaviors, and sensations that are repeated throughout your life.

There are seven core beliefs that are particularly linked to relationship trauma bonding:

- **Abandonment.** This core belief is formed as the result of physical or emotional loss, a lack of emotional support or connection, or an unstable or unreliable environment.

- **Mistrust and abuse.** Childhood experiences that involve abuse (verbal, physical, or sexual), betrayal, humiliation, or manipulation form this core belief. The person with this core belief expects others to hurt, abuse, humiliate, cheat, lie, manipulate, or take advantage of them.

- **Emotional deprivation.** This core belief results from others not adequately meeting the child's emotional needs. There are three forms of emotional deprivation: (1) deprivation of nurturance (the absence of attention, affection, warmth, or companionship), (2) deprivation of empathy (the absence of understanding, listening, self-disclosure, or mutual sharing of feelings with others), and (3) deprivation of protection (the absence of strength, direction, or guidance from others).

- **Defectiveness.** This core belief develops when the child is made to feel like they are defective, bad, unwanted, or inferior in important ways or that others would find them unlovable if their "flaws" were exposed. These flaws may be private (for example, feeling unworthy of love or private sexual desires) or public (such as a physical characteristic or behavior that makes a person feel self-conscious).

- **Dependence.** This core belief develops when a person is made to feel that they are incapable or helpless and require significant assistance from others or that they cannot survive without a specific person (or both).

- **Failure.** This core belief makes a person feel like they are inadequate or incompetent and will ultimately fail. When they compare themselves to others, they feel like a failure. Any successes make them feel like an impostor.

- **Subjugation.** Subjugation is the core belief that the person needs to meet the needs of others at the expense of their own needs to avoid real or perceived consequences. It often results in the person surrendering control to others due to real or perceived coercion.

Each of these beliefs develops as a result of particular childhood experiences you did or didn't have. If you have *abandonment* or *mistrust and abuse* core beliefs, for instance, these likely developed because you weren't provided with a stable and safe environment in your developmental years. You likely lived with the fear that you would be left, you couldn't trust the people who were supposed to take care of you, or you would be physically or emotionally abused. With the abandonment core belief, in particular, you may struggle with the emotional pain associated with thoughts like: *People I love will leave me or die. No one has ever been there for me. The people I've been closest to are unpredictable. In the end, I will be alone.* As for the painful thoughts associated with the mistrust and abuse core belief, these include: *I always get hurt by the people close to me. People will take advantage of me if I don't protect myself. People I trusted have verbally, physically, or sexually abused me.*

An *emotional deprivation* core belief will likely develop if you don't receive love, understanding, empathy, affection, and guidance from caregivers and peers. You will experience the fear that you might never have the connection to others that you desire. The emotional pain associated with the following statements will resonate with you: *I feel lonely. I don't get the love I need. I don't have anyone in my life who really cares about me or meets my emotional needs. I don't feel emotionally connected to anyone.*

If you have a *dependence* core belief, you weren't taught to be autonomous in your formative years. This means that you experience fear when you are faced with having to be self-reliant, having to handle responsibilities alone, or not having anyone to rely on. Painful thoughts might include: *I'm incapable of doing anything alone. I need someone to take care of me because I don't feel like I can take care of myself. I feel like less of an adult when faced with responsibilities.*

Defectiveness and *failure* core beliefs form in the absence of love, acceptance, and respect. Without the support to help you develop self-esteem, you will experience the fear that you will never be good enough. If you have a defectiveness core belief, you would experience painful thoughts such as these: *If people really knew me, they would reject me. I am unworthy of love. I feel shame about my faults. I present a false self because if people saw the real me, they wouldn't like me.* The failure core belief will elicit emotional pain with thoughts like: *Most of my peers are more successful than I am. I am not as smart as other people in my life. I feel ashamed that I don't measure up to others. I don't possess any special talents.*

When you aren't raised in a nurturing environment where you were encouraged to express your needs and desires, you will likely develop a *subjugation* core belief. You will experience the fear and associated pain that you and your needs will never matter as much as others and their needs. Emotionally painful thoughts might include: *I won't be accepted or loved if I don't put the needs and desires of others first. I need the approval of others. I give more than I receive in relationships* (Young and Klosko 1994).

Did you get a sense from these descriptions about the origin of your core beliefs? No worries if you didn't; you will take a self-assessment for each core belief that will shed light on this part of your narrative.

Assessing Your Core Beliefs

Understanding your core beliefs is a big step toward understanding—and ending—your relationship trauma bonds. That said, while the assessments in this section can be very helpful, they are much like GPS navigation—it works well, but sometimes can take you slightly off course. For example, you might score low on a core belief based upon your answers to the statements, but you may feel that you resonate with the definition of the core belief. Trust yourself *and* the assessments!

Choosing the right time to take the self-assessments can also make a difference in the results. It's best to take them when your heart is open and you are feeling emotionally vulnerable. You will get a very different result if you take them when you are feeling shut down or guarded. And through it all, remember that core beliefs are most troublesome when they remain outside of awareness. Shining a light on the ones you might be struggling with is the first step in liberating yourself from the emotional pain that is inherent in a toxic relationship.

Abandonment Core Belief

The abandonment core belief is a perceived instability or unreliability of those on whom you relied for support and connection. It involves the belief that the significant person or people in your life will not be able to provide emotional support, connection, or protection because they are emotionally unstable and unpredictable, unreliable, or erratically present, or will die or abandon you for someone else.

Rate the following statements using the scale below:

1 = completely untrue of me   4 = moderately true of me

2 = mostly untrue of me   5 = mostly true of me

3 = slightly more true than untrue of me   6 = describes me perfectly

I worry a lot that the people I love will die or leave me.   _____

I cling to people because I am afraid they will leave me.   _____

I do not have a stable base of support.   _____

I keep falling in love with people who cannot be there for me in a   _____
committed way.

People have always come and gone in my life.   _____

I get desperate when someone I love pulls away.   _____

I get so obsessed with the idea that my lovers will leave me that   _____
I drive them away.

The people closest to me are unpredictable. One minute they   _____
are there for me, and the next minute they are gone.

I need other people too much.   _____

In the end, I will be alone.   _____

Add up the points from each statement to get your total score. Put a star next to each statement you scored with a 5 or 6.

Total score: _____

Here's how to interpret your total score:

10–19: Very low. This core belief probably does not apply to you.

20–29: Fairly low. This core belief may apply only occasionally.

30–39: Moderate. This core belief is an issue in your life.

40–49: High. This is definitely an important core belief for you.

50–60: Very high. This is a powerful core belief for you.

Note: If you have a low score but you have at least one statement that you rated a 5 or 6, then this core belief is an issue in your life. If you feel like this core belief is significant in your life but your score was lower than you expected, then you might want to consider some of the following childhood situations that could have contributed to your feelings:

- Your home life was unstable.

- You did not have the attention you needed from your parents or caregivers.

- You lost a parent or caregiver.

- You had inconsistent or multiple caregivers.

While your total score can be revealing, it's also important to look at the significance of a core belief if you scored low on most of the statements for that belief but high on one or two. If that happens now or at any point in this chapter, make a note of it. We'll discuss it further at the end of each assessment.

Mistrust and Abuse Core Belief

The mistrust and abuse core belief is often present in RTBs. You may experience the mistrust and abuse core belief if you grew up in an environment in which you didn't trust the person or people close to you, you didn't feel safe, or you were physically, verbally, emotionally, or sexually abused. (Note: If the last of these categories applies to you, take particular care of yourself as you read this book and work through the activities. You may find it helpful to speak to a professional to help you process your experience and care for yourself as you confront your RTBs.)

Rate the following statements using the scale below:

1 = completely untrue of me   4 = moderately true of me

2 = mostly untrue of me   5 = mostly true of me

3 = slightly more true than untrue of me   6 = describes me perfectly

I expect people to hurt me or use me.   _____

Throughout my life, people close to me have abused me.   _____

It is only a matter of time before the people I love will betray me.   _____

I have to protect myself and stay on my guard.   _____

If I am not careful, people will take advantage of me.   _____

I set up tests for people to see if they are really on my side.   _____

I try to hurt people before they hurt me.   _____

I am afraid to let people get close to me because I expect them   _____
to hurt me.

I am angry about what people have done to me.   _____

I have been physically, verbally, or sexually abused by people I   _____
should have been able to trust.

Add up the points from each statement to get your total score. Put a star next to each statement you scored with a 5 or 6.

Total score: _____

Here's how to interpret your total score:

10–19: Very low. This core belief probably does not apply to you.

20–29: Fairly low. This core belief may apply only occasionally.

30–39: Moderate. This core belief is an issue in your life.

40–49: High. This is definitely an important core belief for you.

50–60: Very high. This is a powerful core belief for you.

Note: Again, if you have a low score but you have at least one statement that you rated a 5 or 6, then this core belief is likely an issue in your life. If you feel like this core belief is significant in your life but your score was lower than you expected, then you might want to consider some of the following childhood situations that could have contributed to your feelings:

- You felt like the outsider in your family.

- Your home wasn't a safe environment.

- You couldn't trust anyone in your family.

- Your weaknesses were exploited.

- You were called names.

Emotional Deprivation Core Belief

Emotional deprivation is a common core belief if you grew up in an environment where you didn't receive emotional support, attention, affection, guidance, and understanding.

Rate the following statements using the scale below:

1 = completely untrue of me   4 = moderately true of me

2 = mostly untrue of me   5 = mostly true of me

3 = slightly more true than untrue of me   6 = describes me perfectly

I need more love than I get. _____

No one really understands me. _____

I am often attracted to cold partners who can't meet my needs. _____

I feel disconnected, even from the people who are closest to me. _____

I have not had one special person I love who wants to share themselves with me and cares deeply about what happens to me. _____

No one is there to give me warmth, holding, and affection. _____

I do not have someone who really listens and is tuned in to my true needs and feelings. _____

It is hard for me to let people guide or protect me, even though it is what I want inside. _____

It is hard for me to let people love me. _____

I am lonely a lot of the time. _____

Add up the points from each statement to get your total score. Put a star next to each statement you scored with a 5 or 6.

Total score: _____

Here's how to interpret your total score:

10–19: Very low. This core belief probably does not apply to you.

20–29: Fairly low. This core belief may apply only occasionally.

30–39: Moderate. This core belief is an issue in your life.

40–49: High. This is definitely an important core belief for you.

50–60: Very high. This is a powerful core belief for you.

Note: If you have a low score but you have at least one statement that you rated a 5 or 6, then this core belief is an issue in your life. If you feel like this core belief is significant in your life but your score was lower than you expected, then you might want to consider some of the following childhood situations that could have contributed to your feelings:

- Your caregiver was not tuned in to your needs.

- You didn't feel connected to your caregiver.

- You didn't have anyone solid to rely on.

- You did not feel valued or special.

- You didn't receive physical or verbal affection.

Defectiveness Core Belief

The defectiveness core belief is present and likely drives your relationship choices if you feel that you are bad, unworthy, or defective, and that if someone saw you for who you really are, they would find you unlovable and reject you.

Rate the following statements using the scale below:

1 = completely untrue of me   4 = moderately true of me

2 = mostly untrue of me   5 = mostly true of me

3 = slightly more true than untrue of me   6 = describes me perfectly

No person could love me if they really knew me. _____

I am inherently flawed and defective. I am unworthy of love. _____

I have secrets that I do not want to share, even with the people _____
closest to me.

It was my fault that my parents could not love me. _____

I hide the real me. The real me is unacceptable. The self I show _____
is a false self.

I am often drawn to people—parents, friends, and lovers—who _____
are critical and reject me.

I am often critical and rejecting, especially of people who seem _____
to love me.

I devalue my positive qualities. _____

I live with a great deal of shame about myself. _____

One of my greatest fears is that my faults will be exposed. _____

Add up the points from each statement to get your total score. Put a star next to each statement you scored with a 5 or 6.

Total score: _____

Here's how to interpret your total score:

10–19: Very low. This core belief probably does not apply to you.

20–29: Fairly low. This core belief may apply only occasionally.

30–39: Moderate. This core belief is an issue in your life.

40–49: High. This is definitely an important core belief for you.

50–60: Very high. This is a powerful core belief for you.

Note: If you have a low score but you have at least one statement that you rated a 5 or 6, then this core belief is an issue in your life. If you feel like this core belief is significant in your life but your score was lower than you expected, then you might want to consider some of the following childhood situations that could have contributed to your feelings:

- You were rejected.

- You felt unloved.

- You were blamed when anything went wrong.

- You were compared with others in an unfavorable way.

- You were made to feel like a disappointment.

- You were repeatedly criticized.

Failure Core Belief

If you feel like you've failed, that failure is inevitable, or that you don't measure up to your peers because you aren't as smart, talented, or successful, then you probably have a failure core belief.

Rate the following statements using the scale below:

1 = completely untrue of me   4 = moderately true of me

2 = mostly untrue of me   5 = mostly true of me

3 = slightly more true than untrue of me   6 = describes me perfectly

I feel I am less competent than other people in areas of achievement. _____

I feel that I am a failure when it comes to achievement. _____

Most people my age are more successful in their work than I am. _____

I was a failure as a student. _____

I feel I am not as intelligent as most of the people I associate with. _____

I feel humiliated by my failures in the work sphere. _____

I feel embarrassed around other people because I do not measure up in terms of my accomplishments. _____

I often feel that people believe I am more competent than I really am. _____

I feel that I do not have any special talents that really count in life. _____

I am working below my potential. _____

Add up the points from each statement to get your total score. Put a star next to each statement you scored with a 5 or 6.

Total score: _____

Here's how to interpret your total score:

10–19: Very low. This core belief probably does not apply to you.

20–29: Fairly low. This core belief may apply only occasionally.

30–39: Moderate. This core belief is an issue in your life.

40–49: High. This is definitely an important core belief for you.

50–60: Very high. This is a powerful core belief for you.

Note: If you have a low score but you have at least one statement that you rated a 5 or 6, then this core belief is an issue in your life. If you feel like this core belief is significant in your life but your score was lower than you expected, then you might want to consider some of the following childhood situations that could have contributed to your feelings:

- You felt incapable of living up to the high standards that were set for you.

- You were inferior to your peers.

- You were compared unfavorably with a sibling or peers.

- You didn't learn self-discipline or how to be responsible.

- Your accomplishments were minimized by a parent or caregiver who felt threatened.

Dependence Core Belief

The dependence core belief is present if you believe it would be difficult to survive emotionally without another person and that you would not be able to take care of yourself.

Rate the following statements using the scale below:

1 = completely untrue of me   4 = moderately true of me

2 = mostly untrue of me   5 = mostly true of me

3 = slightly more true than untrue of me   6 = describes me perfectly

I feel less like an adult and more like a child when it comes to _____
dealing with the responsibilities of daily life.

I do not have the capability to get by on my own. _____

I do not cope well by myself. _____

Other people are better at taking care of me than I am at taking _____
care of myself.

If I don't have someone to guide me, I have trouble tackling new _____
tasks.

I can't do anything right. _____

I am inept. _____

I don't have common sense. _____

I do not trust my own judgment. _____

Everyday life is overwhelming to me. _____

Add up the points from each statement to get your total score. Put a star next to each statement you scored with a 5 or 6.

Total score: _____

Here's how to interpret your total score:

10–19: Very low. This core belief probably does not apply to you.

20–29: Fairly low. This core belief may apply only occasionally.

30–39: Moderate. This core belief is an issue in your life.

40–49: High. This is definitely an important core belief for you.

50–60: Very high. This is a powerful core belief for you.

Note: If you have a low score but you have at least one statement that you rated a 5 or 6, then this core belief is an issue in your life. If you feel like this core belief is significant in your life but your score was lower than you expected, then you might want to consider some of the following childhood situations that could have contributed to your feelings:

- Your parents made decisions for you.

- You were given little or no responsibilities.

- Your parents interfered in your decision-making.

- Your opinions and choices were criticized.

Subjugation Core Belief

The subjugation core belief is present when there is the perception that the other person's desires, feelings, and opinions are more important. It can involve surrendering control to others because one fears consequences for failing to do so.

Rate the following statements using the scale below:

1 = completely untrue of me　　　　4 = moderately true of me

2 = mostly untrue of me　　　　　　5 = mostly true of me

3 = slightly more true than untrue of me　　6 = describes me perfectly

I let other people control me and my life.　　　　_____

I worry that if I don't fulfill the wishes of others, they will get　　_____
angry, retaliate, or reject me.

The major decisions in my life are not in my control.　　_____

I have difficulty demanding that other people respect my rights.　_____

I really worry about pleasing people and getting their approval.　_____

I go to great lengths to avoid conflict or confrontations with　　_____
others.

I give more to others than they give to me.　　_____

I experience the pain of other people deeply, which leads me to　_____
take care of the people I'm close to.

If I put myself first, I feel guilty.　　_____

I am a good person because I think of others more than I think　_____
of myself.

Add up the points from each statement to get your total score. Put a star next to each statement you scored with a 5 or 6.

Total score: _____

Here's how to interpret your total score:

10–19: Very low. This core belief probably does not apply to you.

20–29: Fairly low. This core belief may apply only occasionally.

30–39: Moderate. This core belief is an issue in your life.

40–49: High. This is definitely an important core belief for you.

50–60: Very high. This is a powerful core belief for you.

Note: If you have a low score but you have at least one statement that you rated a 5 or 6, then this core belief is an issue in your life. If you feel like this core belief is significant in your life but your score was lower than you expected, then you might want to consider some of the following childhood situations that could have contributed to your feelings:

- Your parents or caregivers controlled your life.
- You were made to feel bad if you didn't do what others wanted.
- Your parents or caregivers used you as a confidant.
- You weren't given a normal amount of freedom.
- You were punished if you didn't agree with your parents.
- You weren't allowed to make your own choices.

That was a lot of information to process. Some of the statements may have felt confronting to you; others may have brought up feelings or memories you struggle with. And you are likely experiencing a mix of emotions as a result—sadness, anger, guilt, anxiety, longing, or loneliness, to name a few. Take some time to acknowledge your experience. How are you feeling after assessing your core beliefs? Did any of the results confirm what you already suspected? Did any of the results surprise you? Have you gotten a little more clarity about how you see yourself and your relationships? Use your journal to write down your responses.

Looking at Your Core Belief Statements

Now, let's take a closer look at the core belief statements that you scored a 3 or higher. Take a moment to jot each of these down in your journal, leaving space after each of the statements so you have room to write down any memories or experiences that are connected to that statement.

Camila

Let's take a look at Camila, who, as you might recall from chapter 1, has an anxious attachment style. Camila scored high on the *abandonment* and *emotional deprivation* core beliefs. She wrote down the statements with the highest scores for each core belief.

Here is her completed exercise for the *abandonment* core belief:

I worry a lot that the people I love will die or leave me. *When my father got deported, it was as if he died because I never saw him again. Even though I had some contact, he couldn't be there for me in the way that I needed him. My mother was a permanent fixture in my life, but she worked so much to support us that I was left feeling that I lost her as well.*

I cling to people because I am afraid they will leave me. *I remember from an early age becoming very attached to my teachers in school. As an adult, I find myself clinging early in relationships, which often alienates the other person.*

I keep falling in love with people who cannot be there for me in a committed way. *I tend to pick women on dating apps who indicate that they're looking for something casual. This always sets me up for disappointment and sadness when I try to push for more.*

I get desperate when someone pulls away. *This is difficult for me to admit, even to myself, the desperate things I've done when someone withdraws from me.*

I get so obsessed with the idea that my lovers will leave me that I drive them away. *As soon as I start dating someone, I do and say things that I would want, but it drives them away.*

Here is Camila's completed exercise for the *emotional deprivation* core belief:

I need more love than I get. *This need feels very deep to me. I know it goes back to my father leaving and my mother being preoccupied with work.*

No one really understands me. *My experience of my father being deported feels unique to me, so I feel like it's difficult for people to understand my trauma. Most of the time I don't share it with others.*

I am often attracted to cold partners who can't meet my needs. *I'm not sure if they're cold or if I want too much. I need to think about this some more.*

I do not have someone who really listens and is tuned in to my true needs and feelings. *I tend to be attracted to women who are very focused on their careers and don't devote a lot of time to activities and relationships outside of work.*

Ian

Now let's look at Ian's scores. While Ian had a low overall score for the *mistrust and abuse* core belief, he did have one statement that he scored a 6. He had high scores on *emotional deprivation* and *defectiveness* core beliefs. Here are the statements and his responses. We'll start with his *mistrust and abuse* core belief statement:

> I am afraid to let people get close to me because I expect them to hurt me. *I don't have any memory of being abused by my parents or any other adult, but I know that I believe this statement. It's painful for me to admit that I act like I don't have time for a relationship—I spend most of my time working—because I am fearful that I'll get hurt. I've been with two women—Phoebe and Daphne—who I saw potential with, but I was unable to move forward.*

Here are Ian's *emotional deprivation* core belief statements:

> I feel disconnected, even from the people who are closest to me. *My parents are still married, and I'm close to them in the sense that I see them frequently. But we've never shared our emotions or anything that feels vulnerable. I know other people do, but it's just not the way I was raised.*

> It is hard for me to let people love me. *When I started having feelings for Phoebe and Daphne and they expressed feelings for me, it made me feel like I was losing control. I didn't know what to do with those feelings, so I stopped dating them.*

> I am lonely a lot of the time. *I have friends and coworkers who I spend time with, but I'm starting to understand that the lack of deeper connection leaves me feeling like I'm alone. I don't know quite how to explain it, but when I'm with my friends I can feel lonely.*

These are Ian's *defectiveness* core belief statements:

It was my fault that my parents could not love me. *I know this thought might seem irrational, but it is my fault that my mom got postpartum depression after giving birth to me. It was me who turned our lives upside down. They never said they didn't love me, and they never blamed me, but everyone knew my mom was fine until I entered their lives.*

I live with a great deal of shame about myself. *My shame is related to my childhood and the negative impact of my birth on my mom. And I feel shame around my inability to make close connections with others.*

One of my greatest fears is that my faults will be exposed. *As I wrote above, I feel shame around my inability to open up to others and make close connections. I'm afraid to tell anyone that I don't know how to do that. I tend to pull away from people or keep our relationship on a superficial level so they won't figure out that I'm not normal in this way. I feel defective.*

Aryan

Let's look at Aryan's core belief statements and his related memories and experiences. Remember, we learned in chapter 1 that he has a secure attachment, but due to the trauma of being responsible for his brother's death, he is trapped in an RTB.

Aryan scored low on the *abandonment* core belief scale, but one of his statements is a 6. If you score low on one of the scales, but you have a high score on a statement, it is important to look at the significance of the statement. As he explains below, it is a significant fear in his life, and that fear influences choices and behaviors, as we'll see when we learn more about Aryan's struggles.

Abandonment core belief statement: I worry a lot that the people I love will die or leave me. (*Score: 6*)

Abandonment-related core belief memory or experience: *My brother, who was my best friend, died when I was in high school and he was in college. I was with him when he died.*

Again, Aryan had a low overall score on the *defectiveness* core belief scale, but he scored high on one statement.

Defectiveness core belief statement: I live with a great deal of shame about myself. (*Score: 6*)

Defectiveness-related core belief memory or experience: *I was driving the car when my brother and I got into a fatal car crash. My brother was home from college over winter break. The roads were icy. My brother told me to slow down, but I didn't listen to him because I was going the speed limit. I was a new driver, so I should have listened to him. If I had, he would still be alive. I live with the shame and guilt every day.*

Aryan scored high on the *dependence* core belief with an overall score of 39. He gave a score of 3 to six of the statements, 5 to three of the statements, and a 6 to one of the statements.

Here are his responses to the highest-scoring dependence core belief statements:

I do not have the capability to get by on my own. *I relied on my brother so much when I was growing up, now without him, I don't feel confident to do it on my own.*

I do not cope well by myself. *This is related to the previous statement. I just don't feel confident dealing with my life on my own.*

If I don't have someone to guide me, I have trouble tackling new tasks. *My brother guided me and advised me from the time I can remember. After he died, I felt even less confident to make decisions on my own. I did everything both of my moms wanted me to do. I rely heavily on my partner to choose how we spend our time, who we hang out with, and nearly everything else.*

I do not trust my own judgment. *This is a very painful reminder that it was my judgment that killed my brother. If I had listened to him and slowed down, he would probably still be alive. Ever since that day, I haven't trusted myself to make a decision. The result is that I give other people in my life more power over my life than I allow myself. I'm in a relationship where I don't have a voice. I am living someone else's life, and I feel trapped.*

As you can see from Aryan's core beliefs, related statements, and memories, it's possible to have a secure attachment and have a traumatic experience (in his case, the death of his brother) in your life that changes how you view yourself, others, and the world around you. The trauma does not have to be a repeated trauma for it to deeply influence your relationships and behavior.

Now, if you haven't already, look back at the statements you wrote down in your journal and see if you can connect each one to memories of events or experiences that created them. Once this is done, you'll have already set the stage for the next exercise.

Core Belief Experiences

What follows is a list of core beliefs and the experiences that inform them. For each experience that formed each core belief, in your journal, write down the name(s) of the people who caused the trauma.

Note: This is not meant to be a blaming exercise. If you're feeling like *I don't want to say my mom caused my trauma because she did the best she could at the time*, that's understandable, and that's not the goal of this exercise. This is designed to get you closer to understanding the source of your core beliefs and their related thoughts and emotions. This provides you with the information you need to identify an individual who might be a potential RTB or toxic person for you. When you have this awareness about the source of your trauma, it will help you avoid types of people who will reinforce your relationship patterns. This will move you in the direction of healthy attachments.

Abandonment:

- Lack of stability
- Died or left
- Unpredictable
- Unreliable
- Erratically present

Mistrust and abuse:

- Hurt me physically
- Hurt me sexually
- Hurt me verbally
- Betrayed me
- Took advantage of me

Emotional deprivation:

- Lack of affection
- Lack of attention
- Lack of emotional support
- Lack of love
- Lack of understanding

Defectiveness:

- Made me feel bad
- Made me feel unworthy
- Made me feel defective
- Rejected me
- Made me feel unlovable

Failure:

- Made me feel like a failure
- Made me feel less than
- Made me feel less smart
- Made me feel less talented
- Made me feel less attractive

Dependence:

- Made me feel incapable
- Made me feel I couldn't cope by myself
- Made me feel like I couldn't survive alone

Subjugation:

- Made me feel like my needs were less important
- Made me feel like there would be consequences if I didn't put their needs and desires first
- Made me give control of my life to them

Do you feel like you gained an increased understanding of what's at play with your core beliefs and the origin, specifically the person or people, associated with your core beliefs? Was there anything that surprised you? Write about the experience in your journal if you like.

Core Beliefs and Attachment Style

Keep the information you learned in the above exercise in mind as we take a look at your attachment style (from the assessment in chapter 1). Let's consider the relationship between your core beliefs and your attachment style, two of the foundational components of who you are and how you make decisions in relationships. Your core beliefs and attachment style often operate outside of awareness, and because of that, they can keep you stuck in an RTB or draw you to toxic people or situations.

Take out your journal and respond to the following questions:

- What is your attachment style? Are you avoidant, anxious, or securely attached?

- How do you think your core beliefs relate to or interact with your attachment style?

- What else do you want to explore about how your core beliefs and attachment style unconsciously guide your choices in relationships?

Moving Forward

In the next chapter, you will bring awareness to the connection between your attachment style, your temperament, your core beliefs, and your behaviors.

This was a significant amount of information to process. Now might be a good time to take a break. While it may be hard to believe, especially if you feel your core beliefs have caused particular havoc in your relationships, remember that core beliefs are ultimately a protective response to the trauma that you experienced. This is because they help you make assumptions and predictions about what will likely happen in a familiar situation. In fact, core beliefs, when triggered, bring up powerful automatic thoughts, emotions, and behaviors, again as a protective response. The trouble starts when we rely on those same thoughts, emotions, and behaviors long past the childhood in which they might have been useful; that's the point when what was once protective becomes maladaptive and cyclical. But with the understanding of your thoughts, emotions, and behaviors that you'll build in this book, you'll be prepared to break your RTBs once and for all.

CHAPTER 3

Trauma-Bonding Coping Behaviors

In this chapter you will be faced with some challenging terrain. This chapter is all about how you cope with the pain associated with your core beliefs. It's likely that you will experience increased feelings of shame as you explore your behaviors and the origin of those behavioral patterns. This is one of the most difficult sections of the path that you're on. But remember, this path will get you closer to the relationships and the life you deserve. And as for the unavoidable shame that will likely get triggered, you are not responsible for what created your trauma. The behaviors that formed as a result of your traumatic experience(s) were protective in nature, and they helped you survive when you were growing up. Now, they are behavioral patterns that no longer serve you. But they can be identified and changed.

By the end of this chapter, you will have a better understanding of how your attachment style, temperament, and core beliefs interact to influence your behavior. While your attachment style and core beliefs can't be eliminated, with awareness, their power can be minimized over time and your behavior can change. And when your behavior changes, your relationship dynamics will change. Identifying and understanding your behaviors is one of many steps along your path that will provide you with the self-awareness, self-compassion, and empowerment to make the necessary changes to free yourself from the shame that's serving as a barrier between you and a healthy connection with others.

Temperament and Coping Styles

In chapter 1, you identified the nine traits that make up your temperament. Understanding your activity level, your distractibility, your response to triggers, your relationship to structure and routine, your sensory sensitivity, how you respond to new things, your ability to adapt, your attention span, and your disposition brings awareness to your temperament. This is important because temperament is directly related to your coping style. In other words, how do you behave when your core beliefs get triggered? What is your coping style in a trauma-bonding relationship? These are patterns of behavior that have developed as a result of your trauma and your unconscious drive to keep yourself safe. How you cope with the fear you experience when you get triggered differs depending upon your temperament.

We've put the nine traits in a grid and marked them according to how Camila, Ian, and Aryan scored themselves. We've used their first initial (C=Camila, I=Ian, A=Aryan). As they bring awareness to their coping behaviors, we will see the intersection between temperament and their coping styles.

Scoring	1	2	3	4	5
Activity level			A	I	C
Distractibility		A	I	C	
Response	I		A	C	
Rhythmicity and regularity		C		I	A
Sensory sensitivity			I/C		A
Response to new things	A	I		C	
Ability to adapt	A		I	C	
Attention span			I/A	C	
Disposition		I	A	C	

Create a blank grid like the one above for yourself in your journal. Looking at your grid will likely trigger increased feelings of shame. The goal of this process is to eliminate the feelings of shame that have been haunting you for too much of your life. In order to break the behavioral patterns that no longer serve you, you need to identify them. Your current behavior is understandable. The trauma that you experienced took away your ability to have a more balanced, less emotional reaction to situations you experience, especially in relationships. This results in additional feelings of shame, which perpetuates the cycle of trauma-bonding relationships. Understanding what drives your behavior will help you make different choices and begin to eliminate the feelings of shame.

Looking at your grid, can you bring some new awareness to how the nine traits that inform temperament have influenced your coping style? Can you make a connection between your temperament and your attachment style? Write about it in your journal.

Here's what Camila wrote: "One of the statements that I scored high on in the attachment assessment was *I often worry that other people won't want to stay with me*. I'm beginning to see how my high energy, intensity, and anxious attachment might be off-putting to some people. I scored high on disposition, so I think, overall, I'm a positive and upbeat person to be around. But I've definitely gotten comments like: 'You really come in hot, and it's going to take someone with a strong personality to handle you.' And I'm realizing that since I'm not good with structure and I like new situations, which I was viewing as a strength, I could come across to some people as being unreliable or not a 'safe' choice as a relationship partner."

Now let's see what Ian wrote: "I scored high on two statements in the attachment assessment that seem important to understanding my behavior in relation to others: *I am uncomfortable when anyone gets too emotionally close to me* and *People often want me to be emotionally closer than I feel comfortable being*. So it makes sense that I have an avoidant attachment. Looking at the nine traits, I think the one that might be related to my inability to get close to others is the response trait. For that one I wrote, 'I'm able to remain calm when faced with an upsetting or triggering situation.' I feel like I was conditioned to remain calm because my mom was incapable of handling an emotional response from me. I always viewed this as a strength because my dad gave me lots of positive feedback. But in my adult life, it's been experienced differently by others. I've gotten comments like, 'You don't seem to care,' or 'You don't seem engaged,' or 'It doesn't seem like you're interested in me.'"

Here's what Aryan wrote: "For the attachment assessment, I scored high on two statements that I'm using for this exercise: *I am comfortable depending on others* and *I am comfortable developing close relationships with others*. That all seems pretty healthy to me. I have a secure attachment. But when I put them with the nine traits that make up my temperament, I'm starting to understand how my temperament could be keeping me stuck. I scored high on sensory sensitivity. I said, 'I react very strongly to changing stimuli in my environment,' and under ability to adapt, I wrote, 'I have difficulty adapting to new situations.' This tells me I don't like change. And I know from my current situation that I will do almost anything to avoid change."

Understanding Your Behavioral Patterns

When you think about your behavioral reactions, you probably can't think of a time that you didn't behave the way you do. That's because your behavior patterns were formed as a result of your trauma. This was your style of coping with the pain associated with your traumatic experiences. And it worked. Your patterns of behavior are automatic and habitual when they operate outside of your awareness. These behaviors might be keeping you stuck in the same relationship dynamic.

Or, maybe you've been unconsciously operating with the goal of creating a different outcome from your original traumatic relationship experience. There is a psychological term for this—it's called "repetition compulsion." It's why you might find yourself unconsciously drawn to a familiar type of person, usually similar to someone who played a role in your traumatic experience. You might find yourself in a similar behavioral experience, or the reenactment of your traumatic experience might be to treat the other person the way that you were treated. This is unconsciously driven by an effort to master or take control of the traumatic experience and create a different outcome. Instead, it reinforces the trauma and increases the feelings of shame (Barkley 2022).

Ultimately, your relationships with your primary caregivers create behavior and relationship patterns that will be unconsciously repeated until those patterns are brought to awareness. In other words, every relationship you have will be cast in the shadow of your trauma until you shine a light on it. And, by shining this light, you are also lighting a path that will lead you to liberation from your relationship trauma bonds.

Before we move on to the next exercise, let's take another look at the core beliefs we've been focusing on and some of the relationship experiences that can trigger them.

- **Abandonment** will likely be triggered if you notice changes in the other person's behavior (for example, in the early stages of the relationship they are texting you often, and then it tapers off); times when the other person is unavailable, with or without an explanation; changes in their mood or affect (for example, they seem annoyed, irritated, distant, detached); they cancel plans or reschedule at the last minute (often with a text); they haven't introduced you to their friends; a disagreement arises without a successful resolution; they start using work as an excuse for why they're unavailable; they don't provide you with reassurance; they discuss future plans that don't include you.

- **Mistrust and abuse** will likely be triggered by any criticism; a raised voice, a change in tone, or any negative affect, especially anger; an interest by another to get to know you on a deeper level (this can be perceived as a way to abuse or manipulate you); any attempts at sexual intimacy that might remind you of past abuse; explained and unexplained times apart; other relationships that you don't understand (such as friendship with an ex).

- **Emotional deprivation** will likely be triggered if you feel like the other person doesn't understand you or isn't interested in understanding you; they don't ask you what you need, or you tell them what you need and they don't meet your need; the connection stays superficial, and there isn't an interest or effort on the part of the other person to make it deeper; they don't express their emotions to you and don't seem interested in your emotions.

- **Defectiveness** will likely be triggered by any criticism; a lack of reassurance, inconsistent reassurance, or conditional reassurance; a desire to get to know you on a deeper level; a belief that the other person saw a part of you that you believe is flawed; expressions of disapproval or disappointment with you.

- **Dependence** will likely be triggered if you are with new people or in a new situation; you must make a decision by yourself; you are faced with a new challenge; someone you rely on isn't there for you.

- **Failure** will likely be triggered if you are being compared or comparing yourself to others; in any situations that make you feel like you don't stack up to the accomplishments, talents, competence, attractiveness, or intelligence of others; when you are with someone who you perceive is better than you; by any criticism; by someone's desire to get to know you.

- **Subjugation** will likely be triggered if you're in a situation or with someone with whom you feel like your needs aren't as important; if another person is trying to control you.

Connecting Core Belief Statements and Triggering Situations

Refer back to your high-scoring core belief statements from the previous chapter. With each statement, identify its relationship to the triggering situations above. Which of these resonated for you? Are there additional triggering situations that relate to each of your core beliefs? Take some time to consider and respond to these questions in your journal.

Now, look at how Camila, Ian, and Aryan completed the exercise.

Camila wrote about the triggering situations related to her abandonment and emotional deprivation core beliefs. As a reminder, Camila scored high on these statements:

- **Abandonment:** *I worry a lot that the people I love will die or leave me. I cling to people because I am afraid they will leave me. I keep falling in love with women who can't be there for me in a committed way. I get desperate when someone pulls away. I get so obsessed with the idea that my lovers will leave me that I drive them away.*

- **Emotional deprivation:** *I need more love than I get. No one really understands me. I am often attracted to cold partners who can't meet* *my needs. I do not have someone who really listens and is tuned in to my true needs and feelings.*

Here's what she wrote: "For abandonment, I'm triggered by any change in texting patterns or not texting back fairly quickly, canceled or rescheduled plans, when they use work as an excuse for not getting together or being out of touch, and when they don't include me in plans with their friends. For my emotional deprivation core belief, I'm triggered when they don't show an interest in getting to know me on a deeper level, when they don't acknowledge my emotions or seem to not care about how I feel, and if they don't tell me how they feel about me—if they're withholding or aloof."

Now, let's look at Ian. He had high-scoring statements for mistrust and abuse, emotional deprivation, and defectiveness.

- **Mistrust and abuse:** *I am afraid to let people get close to me because I expect them to hurt me.*

- **Emotional deprivation:** *I feel disconnected, even from people who are closest to me. It is hard for me to let people love me. I am lonely a lot of the time.*

- **Defectiveness:** *It was my fault that my parents could not love me. I live with a great deal of shame about myself. One of my greatest fears is that my faults will be exposed.*

Here's what Ian wrote about triggering situations that are relevant to him: "I feel like all of mine tie together. For mistrust and abuse, I get triggered when someone makes an effort to get to know me. I feel like it gives them more ways to hurt me. With the emotional deprivation core belief, I get triggered when someone expresses intense emotions. Maybe I'm only experiencing them as intense, but it makes me feel like they expect me to be the same way with them, and that makes me uncomfortable. I get triggered when anyone expresses feelings for me. The defectiveness-related trigger is similar to the mistrust and abuse trigger—anyone trying to get to know me."

Aryan identified the triggering situations related to his abandonment, defectiveness, and dependence core beliefs. These are his high-scoring statements:

- **Abandonment:** *I worry a lot that people I love will die or leave me.*

- **Defectiveness:** *I live with a great deal of shame about myself.*

- **Dependence:** *I do not have the capability to get by on my own. I do not cope well by myself. If I don't have someone to guide me, I have trouble tackling new tasks. I do not trust my own judgment.*

Now, here's what he wrote: "I'm really triggered when I don't get reassurance from my partner, when I hear him talking to one of his friends about plans that don't include me, and any change in mood—those are all related to my abandonment core belief. My defectiveness core belief triggers include receiving criticism and expressions of disapproval or disappointment. For my dependence core belief, I get triggered if I can't reach my partner when I'm dealing with a problem or I need his help with something."

Now, let's look at some of the coping behaviors related to particular core beliefs.

- **Abandonment:** When this core belief is triggered, you might overreact to small things the other person says or does, often believing they are a sign that you will be rejected or abandoned. You have difficulty being away from the other person for an extended period of time. You can never be convinced that your significant other will stay with you. You withdraw or reject in anticipation of being left or rejected. You accuse the other person of wanting to be with someone else, or you are excessively jealous. You are clingy. You avoid intimate relationships because you fear being abandoned or hurt.

- **Mistrust and abuse:** When this core belief is triggered, you might respond with a verbal attack or criticism. You dissociate or withdraw, try to defuse the situation by taking the blame, placate and apologize, or behave in the same way as your childhood abuser.

- **Emotional deprivation:** When this core belief is triggered, you might respond by demanding that your needs be met or become angry that you never get your needs met. You withdraw. You might ask for material objects instead of the love and understanding that you crave.

- **Defectiveness.** When this core belief is triggered, you might hide parts of yourself to avoid exposing your perceived flaws. You put yourself down. You become defensive or hostile when criticized. You become critical of others. You become jealous and possessive. You end a relationship if you feel exposed. You avoid deeper connections.

- **Dependence.** When this core belief is triggered, you might respond by letting others make decisions for you. You become overwhelmed and withdraw. You give up control of the situation to the other. You become angry if others don't help you. You become panicked when faced with making a decision.

- **Failure.** When this core belief is triggered, you might respond by procrastinating. You perform below your potential. You choose to be with people who are less successful than you. You minimize your accomplishments. You exaggerate your mistakes and weaknesses. You focus on one asset (such as your looks) as a distraction from feeling like a failure.

- **Subjugation.** When this core belief is triggered, you might respond by trying to please others. You become angry. You put the needs of others first. You become passive and submissive. You allow the others to take control.

Did you recognize any coping behaviors that are familiar to you? Write them down in your journal. Add any coping behaviors you find yourself engaging in that we haven't listed above. In this next exercise, we're going to put all of this information together.

How do you feel after completing this exercise? Did it help to make the connection between your core beliefs, core belief statements, and triggering situations? So often this connection is never made or it's lost because it's operating unconsciously.

Identifying Your Coping Behaviors

This exercise will provide you with the opportunity to examine the relationship events that are triggering for you. If you are currently dating or in a relationship, draw from that for the exercise. If you're not currently dating, then use your last relationship or dating situation, perhaps the one that prompted you to pick up this book. Once you've identified the relationship event, you'll identify the core belief that was triggered, your automatic coping response, and the outcome—what happens as a result of your behavioral response. At this stage, you can label it a "consequence" because it is getting in the way of moving you closer to a healthy relationship. Understanding how your coping response is keeping you stuck in an RTB is a big step toward change. Let's get started!

In your journal, start by identifying a relationship event. What core belief was triggered? What was your coping response? Finally, write down the outcome or consequence. Repeat this exercise with as many relationship triggering events as you can.

Relationship event:

Core belief triggered:

Coping response:

Outcome or consequence:

Let's see how Camila completed this exercise:

Relationship event: *I don't get a text response from the person I'm interested in. I wait two intolerable hours.*

Core belief triggered: *Abandonment, emotional deprivation.*

Coping response: *I send a follow-up text asking if everything is okay.*

Outcome or consequence: *They either respond with a brief text saying they're busy or they never respond. The bottom line is that my behavior is a turnoff, and it doesn't get me any closer to the relationship I want.*

Here's how Ian completed the exercise:

Relationship event: *I go on a date, and my date asks me questions about myself.*

Core belief triggered: *Mistrust and abuse, emotional deprivation, defectiveness.*

Coping response: *I try to dodge the questions, which makes for an awkward interaction and I suspect makes me come across like I have something to hide.*

Outcome or consequence: *We don't have another date. And I continue to feel lonely.*

Here's how Aryan completed the exercise:

Relationship event: *My partner gets angry at me.*

Core belief triggered: *Abandonment, dependence.*

Coping response: *I apologize and beg him to forgive me.*

Outcome or consequence: *He forgives me, and we go back to the way everything was, but I walk on eggshells to make him happy at the cost of my happiness.*

Were you able to see how easily you fall into unconscious behavioral patterns that at one time protected you and helped you deal with your pain but are now harmful to you and your relationships, thereby causing you more pain? What did you bring to awareness? Write about it in your journal if you like.

Moving Forward

In this chapter, we introduced the role of temperament, triggering situations, and patterns of coping behavior that keep you stuck in RTBs, toxic relationships, and unhealthy attachments. This was a lot of information, and it probably felt challenging to bring awareness to the behaviors that are reinforcing your core beliefs. It can be painful, but you're moving forward. Take some time to reflect on the progress that you've made so far.

When you're ready, the next chapter focuses on the types of people you might find yourself drawn to, strategies they use to exploit your vulnerabilities, and how to guard against being manipulated.

CHAPTER 4

Relationship Trauma-Bond Traps

This chapter will provide you with the information you need to understand how your fear is driving your choices. You might have noticed when you were filling out the assessments that you are still behaving the same way you did in your original trauma relationship. Or you noticed that you have taken on the role, or at least some of the behavioral traits, of the person who traumatized you. Or you noticed that you are drawn to people who are similar to those who caused the original trauma. In all three examples, the result is an RTB. You are either acting as if everyone is the same as the person who traumatized you or picking someone who is like that person. This is understandable.

Our impulse is to seek what we know, what is comfortable, even if it's toxic. It's easier than tolerating the intense feelings that accompany uncertainty and the unknown. After all, we are creatures of habit. So you are unconsciously seeking partners or creating experiences that reinforce the fears that resulted from your trauma. It's likely that these fears have been driving your choices and your behaviors without your awareness. This chapter contains exercises that will help you identify familiar roles and scripts from your childhood that are present in adulthood.

Toxic Types

Let's start by looking at toxic types who trigger and reinforce your core beliefs. One of these types may have caused your original trauma or may represent a type you are drawn to in adulthood.

The abandoner. They are unpredictable with their behavior and their emotions. They appear unstable—they don't seem settled in their career, home, or personal life. They are unavailable—you don't hear from them consistently, and you are unable to reach them with regularity.

The abuser: They will exploit your vulnerabilities, harm you physically or verbally, and abuse you sexually.

The controller: They will expect you to prioritize their needs. They will not respect or prioritize your needs. They will dominate you. They will make you feel guilty if you don't defer to them. They will take away any control you have over your life.

The critic: They will make you feel inferior in every way. They will compare you unfavorably to others, including themselves.

The depriver: They will make you feel unworthy, unloved, and lonely. They will deprive you of the connection that you want.

The devastator: They will exploit your flaws. They will make you feel that you aren't good enough for them. They will make you feel that you don't deserve respect, praise, or appreciation.

Toxic and Triggering Behaviors

Now, let's look at some of the toxic and triggering behaviors you may have experienced. There are many toxic behaviors in dating and relationships. It's likely that you've been subjected to at least one of them. As you read through the list of behaviors below, identify which ones you've experienced. If there are any that you've found yourself particularly vulnerable to in your past or current relationships, make a note in your journal. Also, it's important that you bring awareness to any behaviors that you find yourself engaging in. This might trigger some feelings of shame. But most people have engaged in what we're identifying as toxic behaviors. We'll revisit these in chapter 10 when we discuss new strategies for dating.

Love bombing: This is a form of manipulation where a partner floods you with intense flattery, excessive attention, and affection early on in the relationship so that you become "all in." The goal is to gain control. Once they have your trust and dependence, they will devalue you and ultimately reject you.

Gaslighting: This form of manipulation is designed to create self-doubt by denying your reality. The abuser wants you to feel "crazy" so that they can control you and eventually get you to agree with their version of reality (Conrad 2023).

Ghosting: This behavior involves going radio silent, effectively ending the relationship without acknowledging it or anyone's thoughts or feelings.

Zombie-ing: This is when someone who has ghosted you gets back in touch after an extended period of silence, as if they have come "back to life."

Breadcrumbing: This happens when someone you've dated occasionally gets in touch with you. It might be to keep you on the hook or to give them an ego boost when they need it, without them recognizing the negative impact it can have on you.

Pocketing: This happens when someone keeps the person they are dating separate from their friends or family, "pocketing" them away. You may feel hidden or unwanted, and you may have lots of questions about other parts of their lives they aren't open about with you. While this behavior may not always be toxic, an abuser may engage in pocketing to make you feel insecure and unsure of where you stand.

Groundhogging: This is a behavior pattern where a dater pursues the same "type" of person over and over again, often a "type" that isn't right for them.

Eclipsing: This happens when a partner takes on all your friends, interests, and hobbies. The intention with this behavior could be positive: your partner wants to take an interest in the things and people you care about. However, it's also possible the intention is toxic: your partner wants to blur your personal boundaries, chip away at your autonomy, and become ever-present in your life (Cherelus 2023). Eclipsing may coincide with love bombing.

Toxic Types and Triggering Behaviors

In your journal, connect your experience with toxic types and the triggering behaviors described above with any of your past and current relationships.

Let's hear Joy's story and see how she responded to this exercise about toxic types and behaviors. Joy's father struggled with drug and alcohol addictions. When he was clean and sober, he would live at home with his wife, Joy, and her younger brother. But he would unexpectedly be gone as soon as he started using again. When he was home, he made efforts to be attentive to Joy and give her the love and affection she wanted and deserved. Unfortunately, his addiction often got the best of him, and Joy was left feeling abandoned and longing for the consistent love she so desperately wanted from her father. The assessments in chapters 1 and 2 revealed her anxious attachment style and her abandonment and emotional deprivation core beliefs.

Now, let's look at her responses:

Toxic type: *I am reliably drawn to the* abandoner *who comes on strong. They tell me they've never met anyone like me. They say things that are designed to lead me to believe that we are each other's soulmate. They claim* they want to know everything about me. They seem genuinely interested in my life—past, present, and future. In the beginning, they are in constant touch with me via text during work hours, late night phone calls when we're not together, and dates that include sleepovers.

Toxic behavior: I am vulnerable to almost anyone who uses love bombing. They make me feel like I've finally found someone who wants to know me, understand me, and love me. I believe on a deep emotional level that they are going to fill the void, the unmet need that created my emotional deprivation core belief. Instead, after a short period of time, I have the same feelings of sadness, loneliness, and hopelessness that I felt when my father left. It's devastating.

Toxic type: The controller is compelling to me. I don't see them as a controller. When I meet them, I see them as a strong capable person who would be able to take care of me consistently in a way that my dad never did. But over time, I come to recognize that it's all about them—their needs, their desires—it's their world, and I'm just living in it. I never saw it before, but it fits with my experience with my dad. Even though I didn't view him as the strong type, it was always about him. His life took priority over everyone else's. It's weird that two people who can look so different can make me feel the same way: that my needs don't matter as much as theirs.

It's important to note that while you might be drawn to certain toxic types and toxic behaviors, your engagement with them and your interactions are likely resulting in a toxic loop. In other words, you are *both* behaving and communicating in toxic ways, though to varying degrees. Bringing all of this to awareness is what will provide you with the motivation to use the tools to recognize toxic types and behaviors that have been dominating your life and causing you pain.

How do you feel after identifying the toxic types and behaviors that have been part of your relationships and dating life? Record your response in your journal.

Moving Forward

If you are experiencing shame about any of these toxic behaviors, whether you're on the giving or receiving end, remember that you have been operating from a place of fear. Your past engagement in these patterns is understandable. We are bringing them to awareness so that you recognize what has been keeping you stuck in RTBs and toxic relationships.

In the next chapter, you will gain additional knowledge about why you are drawn to toxic types. You might be asking yourself, *If they're so bad for me, why do I feel such a powerful attachment and such intense emotions?*

CHAPTER 5

Intensity vs. Intimacy

As you've identified the toxic types of people and behaviors that you've experienced or are currently experiencing, you might be confused about how something that started off feeling so good can turn into a relationship trauma bond or toxic relationship. This chapter will help you examine and understand why you are drawn to certain types of people and behaviors that can feel so good in the beginning and yet end so badly.

Remember Joy from the previous chapter? She is vulnerable to *love bombing.* Joy has an emotional deprivation core belief—she received little to no affection or emotional support growing up, or at times she received some, but it was inconsistent. She doesn't have experience with what it feels like to consistently receive expressions of healthy love and affection. So she doesn't recognize the difference between the feeling of true intimacy and high intensity. The intensity that she's mistaking for intimacy is core-belief-driven fear—that she won't receive the love she needs. It feels like an addiction—she can't get enough. And RTBs thrive on intensity; strange as it can seem, the intensity of the fear serves to deepen the bond.

In fact, you may have watched some reality TV shows that demonstrate the power that fear has in bonding people. If you've seen any of the *Bachelor* or *Bachelorette* shows, you know that they often arrange a date for a couple that requires them to do something scary together (such as bungee jumping, skydiving, swimming with sharks, to name a few). Their anxiety and fear are pushed to an all-time high. They do the scary thing together, and they survive. Well, they not only survive, but it actually brings them closer. The fear deepens their bond, and it intensifies their attachment. It's easy to understand why you might be unconsciously addicted to such intense feelings.

Try thinking for a second about the opposite dynamic: Have you had the experience where you meet a nice person, they look great on paper and in person, but you just don't feel it? They don't give you butterflies; you aren't obsessively thinking about them or waiting to hear from them. You enjoy them, but there's no chemistry. After a few dates, or maybe one date is enough for you to decide, you tell them that you're looking for different things, or you just don't feel a romantic connection there. Sometimes, your instincts about a mismatch will be correct—but it's also likely, especially if you struggle with the attachment style and core beliefs that can predispose you to RTBs, that you've passed on getting to know someone who you could build a connection with and create true intimacy. If, as a child, you didn't experience healthy attachment and love, it makes sense that you are confused about what it looks like and how it should feel. While you should trust your instincts, it's also important to bring awareness to and experiment with the unknown, which in this case, might be a healthy alternative to the core-belief-driven types you are typically drawn to and have chemistry with.

The Core of Your Confusion About Love

We're back to your core beliefs. As you know from chapter 2, when we did our deep dive into core beliefs and you took the self-assessments, these beliefs were formed because crucial elements were missing from your childhood and the relationship between you and your caregivers. You didn't receive everything you needed and deserved—safety, love, acceptance, understanding, empathy, affection, guidance, independence—and in their absence, you experienced high levels of anxiety and fear, which drove you to assuage these feelings however you could. Your early relationships and environment, which formed your core beliefs and attachment style, created a template for your future relationships. While it might not make sense rationally, you're likely drawn to or feel a "known" connection with:

- An unstable or unreliable person or environment if you have an abandonment core belief

- Someone who hurts, betrays, or manipulates you if you identify with the mistrust and abuse core belief

- Someone who lacks warmth, empathy, attention, and affection if you have an emotional deprivation core belief

- A person who makes you feel flawed, unworthy, bad, or inferior if you have a defectiveness core belief

- Someone who makes you feel incapable or helpless if you have a dependence core belief

- Someone who brings out your feelings of inadequacy and incompetence if you have a failure core belief

- A person whose wants and needs take priority over yours if you have a subjugation core belief.

While these partners take different forms (gender, hair color, height, career, and so forth) and present in a way that is unique to them, you will find that when you dig deeper, they resemble a caregiver or create an environment that is reminiscent of your formative years.

Bringing Your Past into the Present

In your journal, write about an experience or incidents from your past that were defining moments for you. If this is going to trigger overwhelming emotions, you should consider doing it with your therapist or a trusted friend who is equipped to help you through the process.

To better illustrate this idea, let's look at Amber's story.

Amber grew up in a household that was filled with tension. Her mother, two brothers, and Amber walked on eggshells around her father. He worked in an automobile factory, so his work schedule was predictable, unlike his mood. When he got home from work, he wanted to sit in his recliner, drink one of the four beers he consumed nightly, and watch the news and sports on TV. He was intolerant of the typical noise and behavior that one would expect in a family with three children. Amber observed the way her mother accommodated her father, and she mirrored this behavior.

When Amber's two older brothers inevitably fought, their father often broke up the fight by taking his belt off and whipping them. While Amber had never been subjected to the harsh punishment, she was a frequent witness. Her mother made every effort to stop her sons from misbehaving before their father reached his limit. Unfortunately, Amber experienced her mother as loving and compassionate, so she felt safe sharing a traumatic experience with her: Amber's oldest brother had abused her. Unfortunately, Amber didn't receive the love and understanding she expected from her mother; instead, she told Amber that she needed to forget it ever happened and never speak of it again, because if her father ever found out, he would kill her brother.

Connecting Your Core Beliefs with Your Past Experiences

Identify the core beliefs and related statements that are tied to the experience or incidents that you wrote about above. Record them in your journal.

Now, let's look at the messages that Amber received from her family and environment. Here's what she wrote: *I have an* abandonment *core belief. These are the statements that resonate with me:* The people closest to me are unpredictable. One minute they are there for me, and the next minute they are gone. *I felt this in several ways. My relationship with my mom changed drastically when I told her that my brother abused me. We never spoke about it again, and she acted as if it never happened. It felt like she abandoned me…at least emotionally. And, while my father never hit me, his moodiness created an unpredictable environment.*

Statements that are relevant from my mistrust and abuse *core belief:* I have been physically, verbally, or sexually abused by people I should have been able to trust. *Obviously, this is related to the experience I had with my oldest brother.*

My home wasn't a safe environment, and I couldn't trust anyone in my family are two statements that are true for my experience. Physically, there were constant threats, between my dad's temper and my brothers' fighting. And, after my brother abused me, I never felt safe. I always locked my bedroom door, which is crazy to think about when your home is supposed to be the one place where you should feel safe. And after I shared my experience with my mom and she reacted the way she did, I never felt emotionally safe, and I knew I couldn't trust her.

A statement that resonates with me that is associated with my defectiveness *core belief is* I live with a great deal of shame about myself. *I think when my mom didn't validate my experience and instead made me feel like sharing my experience was going to create a problem for my brother, who was the one who abused me, it made me feel like the bad one. And I also was left feeling like my mom chose my brother over me. So, what's wrong with me?*

Two statements from my subjugation *core belief are* I worry that if I don't fulfill the wishes of others, they will get angry, retaliate, or reject me, *and* The needs, safety, and well-being of others mattered more than mine. *I felt like my mom put me in a bind by telling me that if my dad found out, he would kill my brother. So, I felt I had to essentially put my brother's well-being over my own, even though he had caused me immense harm.*

In summary, Amber's environment was unpredictable, unsafe, lacked emotional support, and made her feel that something was wrong with her and that her needs were less important than the needs of others. While your story might be different from Amber's, you also have an experience that resulted in messages that were internalized and are driving your partner choices and relationship dynamics.

Let's go back to Amber's story to illustrate the patterns that are often created unconsciously.

As an adult, Amber's partner choices were operating outside of her awareness. Because her partners looked different, had different careers, different backgrounds, and different interests, she didn't see that they all had one thing in common: they all reinforced her beliefs about herself, others, and her environment. She was unconsciously drawn to a similar situation that was replicating the original trauma. Amber was stuck in a *repetition compulsion.*

A repetition compulsion is the *unconscious* need to reenact early traumas. You are unknowingly drawn to a similar person(s) or environment as your original trauma. It results in similar painful experiences, and it reinforces your core beliefs. This drive might be an unconscious effort to gain mastery or control over a situation that was out of your control when the original trauma occurred. You were a child then, and you are an adult now. Or you might be unconsciously drawn to the traumatic or toxic environment because it is "known" to you, and that can feel more comfortable than the fear of the unknown. This also makes it easier for you to excuse toxic behavior and remain in a trauma bond. Whatever the unconscious drive is, it's crucial to your healing that you bring it to awareness so that you can break free of trauma bonds and make conscious, healthy choices.

We've all heard statements similar to: "Every girl I've ever dated has cheated on me." "Every guy I've been with has lied to me." "Every person I get close to betrays me." These statements are indicative of a pattern. While you might become aware of similar aspects to the people you date or partner with, you might still be unconsciously drawn to a type of person or environment. By bringing awareness to the qualities that are inherent in a relationship marked by intensity, you can begin to break the cycle of your unconscious drive to replicate your past.

In *The Betrayal Bond*, Patrick J. Carnes (2019) makes a clear distinction between intensity and intimacy. An *intense* relationship is often marked by a feeling of lack of control, instability, volatility, sharp highs and sharp lows, and a general lack of structure or consistency. It can feel exciting and addictive, and also dangerous; you might have a sense of the relationship's tenuousness and stress that distresses you as much as it might compel you. An intimate relationship, by contrast, is marked by mutuality and respect; a degree of sincere and mutual passion; genuine vulnerability—that is, vulnerability that occurs in a context of mutuality and emotional safety; commitment and stability; patience; openness and no secret-keeping; the acknowledgment and negotiation of needs; and healthy conflict resolution.

Which of these templates have your relationships tended to fall into? Respond to the questions below in your journal, writing about your experiences, including the name of the person(s) they occurred with.

1. Have you had relationships in which you were a survivor of abuse and lacked control?

2. Did you experience fear and arousal or a lack of safety?

3. Have you had relationships in which one of you was in when the other was out? That is, was there a lack of stability?

4. Were there threats of betrayal and abandonment in any of your relationships?

5. Have any of your partners used high drama to manipulate and control you or exert control in the situation?

6. Have you had relationships in which there was no structure or rules—relationships that lacked consistency?

7. Was there ever high distraction (another sign of lack of stability)?

8. Have you had relationships that lacked open communication—relationships in which secrecy and mistrust dominated?

9. What about relationships in which conflict escalated beyond reason—where there was a lack of healthy resolution and communication?

10. Have any of your relationships been marked by "break-up and make-up" cycles—by fear and anxiety (which are signs of increased trauma bonding)?

All of these questions describe experiences of intensity in a relationship. How do you feel after writing down your experiences? Does it change how you view those feelings?

Let's look at how Amber answered these questions.

1. Have you had relationships in which you were a survivor of abuse and lacked control? *I am currently with a partner who regularly blames me for our issues.*

2. Did you experience fear and arousal or a lack of safety? *I shared my childhood trauma with him, and he used the information to shame me when he was mad at me.*

3. Have you had relationships in which one of you was in when the other was out? That is, was there a lack of stability? *Yes. Every time I've tried to end the relationship, he promised that he would change and begged me to stay. I did, and he would be more loving for a while, but then everything went back to the way it was before.*

4. Were there threats of betrayal and abandonment in any of your relationships? *Yes. When I've shared my fear of abandonment, it has always been used to control me when there are problems in our relationship.*

5. Have any of your partners used high drama to manipulate and control you or exert control in the situation? *Yes. It often happens when they've been drinking.*

6. Have you had relationships in which there was no structure or rules—relationships that lacked consistency? *Yes, my relationships have always been with people who are unpredictable and inconsistent.*

7. Was there ever high distraction (another sign of lack of stability)? *There's always some drama—an ex who is back in touch or drama at their work or with their family.*

8. Have you had relationships that lacked open communication—relationships in which secrecy and mistrust dominated? *I've often shared my secrets with the hope that the other person will share their secrets with me, but it rarely happens. There's always been locked phone screens and other signs that they have something to hide.*

9. What about relationships in which conflict escalated beyond reason—where there was a lack of healthy resolution and communication? *Yes. We have a big blowup, we avoid discussing the real issues, and we often "make up" by going out and getting drunk together.*

10. Have any of your relationships been marked by "break-up and make-up" cycles—by fear and anxiety (which are signs of increased trauma bonding)? *Yes.*

How do you feel after writing down your experiences? "This was a very eye-opening exercise for me. I didn't realize how many aspects of my romantic relationships related to the experiences and feelings from my childhood." Does it change how you view those feelings? "I recognize how much my choices and behavior were influenced by my early experiences and trauma. I wasn't aware of the connection. Now I have a better understanding about why I feel so stuck."

In *The Body Keeps the Score*, Bessel van der Kolk (2015) makes a clear distinction between the right and left sides of the brain as it relates to trauma. You've likely heard of or learned about the differences between the right and left sides of the brain. The attributes of the right side include emotional, visual, intuitive, and tactual. The left brain's attributes are analytical, linguistic, and sequential, and people who are left-brain types are more rational and logical. Artistic and intuitive people are referred to as right-brain types. For our purposes, this is important because research has shown that when a situation, experience, or person reminds someone of their trauma, the brain reacts as if the trauma is happening in the present. The left side of the brain goes "offline"—that's the logical, rational half of the brain—and the emotional right side of the brain takes control.

This explains an overreaction to a triggering event, but it also explains why you feel the intensity with some people and not with others. The familiar type of person or people you associate with your trauma are going to activate the right side of your brain, elevating your emotional response. It's why you might describe your experience with that person as feeling like you've known each other forever. It's intense, it's known, it's familiar, and it's comfortable. And that is why it's easy to get stuck in a trauma bond or a toxic relationship.

Patrick J. Carnes (2019) explains in his book *The Betrayal Bond* that it's difficult for the rational, logical side of the brain to compete with the emotional side, but by bringing attention to the difference between intensity, which is connected to your trauma bond, and intimacy, you can make choices that will move you toward the healthy attachments you deserve. To that end, let's look at the characteristics inherent in an intimate relationship. It might be more difficult for you to relate to the qualities in an intimate relationship. You might have experienced some of them through friendships. Do your best to share your experiences and the name of the person(s) next to each description in your journal.

1. Have you experienced relationships that were mutual and respectful?

2. Have you experienced relationships in which there was both passion and vulnerability, and both were safe to express?

3. Have you experienced relationships in which there was emotional safety?

4. Have you experienced relationships that were committed and enduring—relationships marked by stability?

5. Have you had relationships in which you've experienced safety and patience? That is, you knew from the way the other person behaved that it was safe for you to have emotions, and the other person was patient enough with you to allow you to feel what you felt and be who you were?

6. Have you had relationships in which you experienced healthy communication and conflict resolution?

7. Have you experienced relationships that were stable enough that there was what you'd consider to be a level of high growth? That is, both you and the other person were able to grow, change, and be different than you'd been, without the relationship itself being thrown into peril?

8. Have you had relationships in which there were no secrets and no need to keep them—you were safe enough with the other person to be able to be honest with them?

9. Have you had relationships in which there was clear acknowledgment and mutual negotiation of needs?

10. Have you had relationships marked by lasting constancy and security?

How do you feel after responding to these questions? If you found it difficult to connect your relationship experience to any or most of them, don't feel bad. These are aspirational. The important takeaway from this exercise is to bring awareness to the gap between a relationship trauma bond and a healthy relationship. One is characterized by and thrives on intensity, and the other grows and thrives on intimacy.

Let's look at Amber's responses:

1. Have you experienced relationships that were mutual and respect-ful? *My best friend from college and my boss.*

2. Have you experienced relationships in which there was both passion and vulnerability, and both were safe to express? *I can be emotionally vulnerable with my best friend, but there isn't passion. I haven't had both in an intimate relationship.*

3. Have you experienced relationships in which there was emotional safety? *Only with my best friend.*

4. Have you experienced relationships that were committed and enduring—relationships marked by stability? *I've been with my partner for two years, but there are constant threats by both of us to end it.*

5. Have you had relationships in which you've experienced safety and patience? That is, you knew from the way the other person behaved that it was safe for you to have emotions, and the other person was patient enough with you to allow you to feel what you felt and be who you were? *I might have felt that in the beginning with my partner, but once I started sharing more of my feelings because I thought it was safe, he dismissed them or minimized them, especially as they related to my experience in our relationship.*

6. Have you had relationships in which you experienced healthy communication and conflict resolution? *I have that with my best friend. We can talk things out in a healthy and productive way. And I feel like I communicate in a healthy way at work. I tried with my partner, and I can at times, but I find myself defaulting to unhealthy and unproductive communication, like yelling or withdrawing.*

7. Have you experienced relationships that were stable enough that there was what you'd consider to be a level of high growth? That is, both you and the other person were able to grow, change, and

be different than you'd been, without the relationship itself being thrown into peril? *I have this with my best friend. We have supported each other unconditionally since we became friends.*

8. Have you had relationships in which there were no secrets and no need to keep them—you were safe enough with the other person to be able to be honest with them? *Yes, with my best friend. I tried with my partner, but my secrets were used to manipulate me.*

9. Have you had relationships in which there was clear acknowledgment and mutual negotiation of needs? *Yes, with my best friend.*

10. Have you had relationships marked by lasting constancy and security? *Yes, with my best friend.*

How do you feel after responding to these questions? *It makes me feel sad that I haven't had and don't have a partner who can provide the qualities of an intimate relationship. At the same time, I feel grateful that I have someone in my life who I have a healthy relationship with. I would like to find it with a partner.*

Moving Forward

You might be feeling overwhelmed by the large gap between the two: the intensity that you have associated with a strong connection and the intimacy that is the true hallmark of a strong connection. And you might be wondering how you are going to make the transition from an RTB to a healthy relationship. In the next chapter, you will learn about some of the tools that will help you break free from trauma bonds and toxic relationships and develop the healthy attachments that you desire and deserve.

CHAPTER 6

What You Value

The previous chapters were designed to bring awareness to how your past trauma, related core beliefs, memories, and triggers have been guiding your choices and keeping you stuck in relationship trauma bonds (RTBs). If you're in a trauma bond, you are constantly living in the past while putting your energy toward surviving as you did during your original trauma. It makes sense that you are distracted from living a value-driven life. Bringing awareness to your painful experiences and understanding their source are essential to making the break from letting your past control you. Now what? How do you navigate your life and create healthy attachments going forward?

Imagine that you are driving a car and you have limited visibility, and you have three passengers piled in the backseat who are giving you directions. Your backseat drivers might shout at you with statements like: "Hurt them before they hurt you!" "Avoid relationships! You'll only get hurt!" "Don't be vulnerable! They will use it against you!" "They haven't texted you back! Don't wait for a response! Text them that you're done." You get the point: none of these statements are helpful. In fact, they are statements generated from your core beliefs, and they've been guiding you since they were formed in your childhood. In the beginning, they may have provided you with helpful directions to keep you safe, but they've outlived their usefulness, and now they're getting in the way.

Now, imagine picking up another passenger. This passenger rides in the passenger seat next to you. They are going to guide you away from the unnecessarily painful life that is inherent in RTBs and toxic relationships. You will be moving toward a life that is guided by your values with the goal of creating and maintaining healthy attachments. All those backseat drivers are still there—ultimately, there's no getting rid of them once they're onboard—but the more you listen to your guide in the front seat and let them help you determine what to do, the softer their voices will get, making it easier to ignore them over time.

You are making a big shift from your automatic coping behaviors, which you identified in chapter 3, and your RTB traps, which you identified in chapter 4, to your values—what matters to you most. It's likely that you've lost sight of them because you've been in survival mode. It makes sense. You shouldn't feel any shame or regret about the choices you felt you had to make to keep yourself safe. But now is the time to draw your attention to what matters to you, what you value, and who you want to be. Each time you respond with a value-driven behavior instead of a core-belief-driven behavior, you will eliminate the pain caused by your unhelpful behaviors.

Below is a list of values with definitions and explanations designed to assist you in choosing the ones that will be most helpful to you. Your values are a guide for how you want to behave, how you want to treat others, how you want to treat yourself, and how you want others to treat you as you attempt to get your needs met in relationships.

Identifying Your Values

The following is a list of values and their definitions. Some definitions are followed by a brief explanation of how that value plays out in relationships. Read each value below, and if it resonates with you, make a note in your journal describing how this value will serve you.

Acceptance: *Recognizing a process or condition without attempting to change or protest it.* If you are in an RTB or toxic relationship, you often stay stuck because you believe that the other person or the situation will change. Accepting the reality that you can't change someone else is an important part of the process of letting go of the relationship.

Appreciation: *A feeling of gratitude and understanding for a situation or person.* When you bring awareness to what you appreciate about your partner, you will be able to better determine if they are a good match for you. In a healthy relationship, you will also feel appreciation for who you are and what you contribute to your partner.

Assertiveness: *The ability to advocate for one's emotions and beliefs with confidence.* If you are in an RTB or toxic relationship, you may find it difficult to be assertive and instead submit to your partner's desires and whims.

Balance: *Stability in one's thoughts, feelings, and priorities.* While this book is focused on liberating yourself from toxic relationships with others, it is equally important to find balance in your life and relationship with yourself.

Belonging: *The feeling of being accepted by and part of a community.* If you are in an RTB or toxic relationship, your sense of belonging may be insecure. Your anxious attachment style may lead to an unstable sense of belonging.

Closeness: *Intimacy and connection between people.* Closeness is an important value to maintain in a healthy relationship.

Commitment: *Dedication to yourself and others.* Both partners in a healthy relationship demonstrate commitment to each other and their connection.

Compassion (for self and others): *An understanding of the suffering and distress experienced by yourself and others.* Compassion is a key ingredient in healthy relationships with yourself and with others. Compassion helps us see others as being similar to ourselves. Compassion also helps us treat ourselves with the same kindness with which we treat our loved ones.

Connection: *A bond between people based on commonalities.*

Curiosity: *An openness and desire for new knowledge and experiences.*

Dependability: *The ability to be relied on and to show up with consistent behavior and reactions.* Toxic relationships often feel intense because your partner is not dependable and exhibits surprising behavior. While this can feel exciting at times, it can contribute to your anxiety.

Discipline: *The ability to focus and exercise self-control.*

Empathy: *The ability to understand and appreciate the emotions and experiences of others.*

Expressiveness: *The ability to feel and share one's emotions easily.*

Fearlessness: *Lacking fright or dread when facing challenges.* Leaving an RTB takes fearlessness and confidence.

Flexibility: *The ability to adjust to changing circumstances and priorities.*

Focus: *Directed awareness of or attention to a topic or situation.*

Friendship: *A connection based on shared values, hobbies, and experiences.*

Gratitude: *The quality of being thankful; readiness to show appreciation for and to return kindness.*

Growth: *Development and change.* Through your path out of toxic attachments, you will experience immense personal growth. While toxic relationships often stifle growth, healthy relationships promote it.

Health: *Physical, mental, emotional, and social well-being.*

Hopefulness: *Optimism about a situation or circumstances.* When you've been stuck in RTBs or toxic relationships, it's easy to feel as if you'll never be in a healthy relationship. It's important that you be hopeful. It is possible. It can happen.

Individuality: *Aspects of one's self that distinguish you from others.* A toxic partner may chip away at who you are without them. As you heal, you will get back in touch with your individuality.

Insightfulness: *A keen ability to understand a situation.* Liberating yourself from an RTB requires that you have deep insight into your values and desires and how those are not being fulfilled.

Integrity: *The quality of being honest and living a values-driven life.*

Intimacy: *Emotional or physical closeness that promotes a bond between people.* Various forms of intimacy are important to maintain a healthy connection. If you are in an RTB or toxic relationship, it is easy to mistake intensity for intimacy.

Kindness: *The quality of being friendly, generous, and considerate; having a pleasant disposition and concern for others.* When seeking a healthy romantic relationship, look for loving-kindness as a key attribute in a partner.

Love: *Deep adoration for and affection toward another person.* Love is a central tenet of an intimate relationship.

Loyalty (to self and others): *Firm and constant support or allegiance to a person.* In an RTB, loyalty to a toxic partner can keep you stuck with them through challenge and abuse, even though they likely don't deserve your loyalty. Loyalty needs to be directed to yourself.

Mindfulness: *Bringing awareness to your experience, thoughts, and feelings.* Prioritizing mindfulness will help you get in touch with your experience of an RTB. This is a highly effective tool where you pay attention to the messages that you receive through all your senses. We will dig into this further in chapter 8.

Openness: *The extent to which you let people and new experiences into your life.* Not all relationships grow stronger when you let people in, but those who are worthy of you will accept you, and you'll know to invest relationship energy into them.

Patience: *The capacity to accept or tolerate delay, trouble, or suffering without getting angry or upset.* In an RTB, your patience will be tested again and again.

Perseverance: *The ability to push through challenging circumstances to meet a goal.* Breaking your patterns when it comes to relationships will be challenging, but the result of lasting and loving connections is worth it.

Presence: *The state of existing, occurring, or being present in a place or thing.*

Reliability: *The ability to be consistent.*

Resilience: *The ability to stay strong through challenging circumstances.*

Respect (for self and others): *Pride and confidence in oneself and others; a feeling that one is behaving with honor and dignity.* If you are in an RTB, it's likely that your partner is not demonstrating respect toward you, and you are not respecting yourself.

Responsibility: *Accepting the duty to deal with something; being accountable; the ability to act independently; a moral obligation to behave correctly and accept the blame when you don't.* Responsibility is key in any relationship, and toxic partners often do not take responsibility for their actions—instead, they turn the blame on you.

Self-control: *The ability to manage one's emotions and behaviors to avoid negative consequences.*

Self-reliance: *The ability to take care of and depend on oneself.* This might be a challenging value for someone with a dependence core belief.

Stability: *Consistency in a situation or circumstance.* This is a hallmark of a healthy relationship.

Strength: *The ability to withstand pressure or challenges.*

Thoughtfulness: *Displaying care or concern for others.*

Trust: *Reliance on one's own honesty and truthfulness.* This will be a challenging, yet worthy, value for someone with a mistrust and abuse core belief.

Understanding: *Awareness of situations and of the thoughts and feelings of yourself and others.*

Willingness: *Openness to new experiences, points of view, or ways of doing things.* This is an important value as you make efforts to break free of toxic patterns.

How did it feel to get in touch with what matters to you and who you want to be? You might have experienced some powerful emotions. Write them in your journal.

To highlight the difference between being guided by the fearmongers in the backseat of your car and the passenger who is leading you toward what matters, we are going to take a look at your current coping behaviors, which you identified in chapter 3, along with the triggering people and experiences you identified in chapter 4. Then, you will identify a value that you would like to choose when triggered and a valued intention (the behavior related to the value).

Exercise: Determining Valued Directions

Start by writing down a triggering event, your coping behavior in reaction to that event, and the negative outcome or consequence.

Triggering event:

Coping behavior:

Negative outcome or consequence:

Now, write down the triggering event and link it to a value or values and the value-driven intention that you would use in place of your current coping behavior and the positive outcome or reward.

Triggering event:

Value(s):

Value-driven intention:

Positive outcome or reward:

Remember Joy? Joy has an anxious attachment style. As an adult, she deals with feelings of sadness, loneliness, and hopelessness that stem from her father abandoning her as a child. Let's look at how she responded to this exercise:

Triggering event: *I was given the opportunity to present at a conference on findings from a big research project at work. I saved several seats in the auditorium for friends and the person I was newly dating. My presentation was well received, and my boss was very complimentary. When the event finished, I walked out only to find out that my new love interest hadn't shown up. My friends congratulated me, but I was very disappointed my date didn't come.*

Coping behavior: *I couldn't even feel happy about my friends' support or my professional success. I shut everyone out and felt completely dejected. I cut the evening short and went home.*

Negative outcome or consequence: *My friends were upset with me for not appreciating their presence and for letting someone I barely knew ruin my experience. I didn't get to fully enjoy what was a big moment in my career.*

Now, reevaluate the triggering event, and this time, link it to a value or values and the value-driven intention that you would use in place of your current coping behavior, and the positive outcome or reward of focusing on that intention. Here are Joy's responses:

Value(s): *Gratitude and self-respect.*

Value-driven intention: *To behave in ways that show my friends and support system that I appreciate them and I'm grateful for their support. To behave in ways that demonstrate that I have self-respect and I deserve to celebrate the moments when I accomplish large and small things.*

Positive outcome or reward: *I focus on what I am grateful for and how I deserve to be treated. I have a positive and uplifting experience with my friends, and I get to celebrate my achievement.*

Now, let's look at Ian's experience with this exercise. You met him in previous chapters. It's relevant to keep in mind that he struggles with building relationships as a result of his avoidant attachment style, his temperament, and his core beliefs. Here's how he responded:

Triggering event: *I was invited to go out with a group of coworkers. We went to a bar near our office. There were lots of people my age, which should have been fun and an opportunity for me to meet and connect with my coworkers as well as with new people.*

Coping behavior: *After what seemed like an eternity of sitting at a table with my coworkers drinking my beer, smiling, and trying to act like I was engaged in the conversation, I excused myself from the table to use the restroom. Then I just left without saying good-bye.*

Negative outcome or consequences: *The next day at work, my coworkers joked endlessly about my "Irish good-bye" and how they'd have to accompany me to the restroom the next time we went out. I was so embarrassed and ashamed that I behaved that way. Especially with people who I see every day at work. It was such a stupid and impulsive move.*

Now let's look at how Ian reevaluated the triggering event and this time, linked it to a value or values and the value-driven intention that he would use in place of his current coping behavior, and the positive outcome or reward of focusing on that intention (McKay, Lev, and Skeen 2012).

Value(s): *Connection, fearlessness, and integrity.*

Value-driven intention: *To join my coworkers for their weekly after-work get-together at the local bar and to push myself to share a small part of myself each time. And to find out more about them. I will not leave our gathering without saying good-bye.*

Positive outcome or reward: *By slowly building connections with my coworkers, they will become my work friends and then maybe my friends.*

How do you feel after doing this exercise? Can you imagine yourself getting closer to a value-driven life?

It's important to note that sometimes the only reward will be living your values and continuing to be the person you want to be as you move further away from being the person who was controlled by fear. You might still get hurt, you might still get treated poorly, but you will recognize your experience and begin to understand that this is all part of life. You will see that by responding with your values in mind, you are no longer creating additional pain for yourself and others. This is a reward in and of itself.

Do this exercise for as many triggering events as you identified in the previous chapters. The process of determining values-based intentions and actions to replace instinctive, fear-driven coping behaviors will give you a map for making choices that serve your goal of letting go of trauma bonds and toxic relationships and developing healthy attachments.

Moving Forward

Now that you've explored your values and how to use them to guide your choices and decisions, let's explore how you can communicate your values, among other important aspects of yourself, to others effectively. In the next chapter, we'll discuss blocks to effective communication as well as key skills to have more successful conversations to get your needs heard and met.

CHAPTER 7

End Toxic Communication

Communication patterns and dynamics are established at an early age. You model what you observe in your family. Through trial and error, you determine how you need to communicate to receive the love and attention you desire and avoid negative or unwanted attention. And, as with your behavior, the communication you've cultivated over the years has likely become a predictable pattern now—one that keeps you stuck in relationship trauma bonds and toxic relationships.

If you have an *abandonment* core belief, you might have avoided sharing any thoughts or feelings that you worried would drive someone away. And if you have a *mistrust and abuse* core belief, it's likely that you didn't feel safe enough to express yourself. With an *emotional deprivation* core belief, you might not have had someone who would listen to you, someone who cared, or someone who had the time to devote to understanding you. And with a *defectiveness* core belief, you likely limited your communication to avoid rejection. If you have a *dependence* core belief, it's likely that you don't trust yourself because from an early age, you received the message that you weren't capable and you needed others to help you and guide you. Someone with a *failure* core belief might be reluctant to express themselves for fear of being compared to others. If you have a *subjugation* core belief, you prioritized the thoughts and feelings of others ahead of your own. In all these ways, our core beliefs steer our impulsive, instinctive reactions to what we encounter.

In this chapter, you will identify your communication patterns and bring awareness to the obstacles they create. Then, you will learn how to effectively communicate your thoughts and feelings with the goal of creating and maintaining healthy attachments.

Again, it's likely that much of your trauma was due to the messages you received from caregivers and others around you—both verbal and nonverbal. In chapter 2, you identified your core beliefs. These beliefs— the products of the messages you've received—have been, until now, unconsciously guiding your choices and negatively impacting your relationships. In turn, you have been communicating these messages and beliefs about yourself to others. Consciously or unconsciously, you are communicating to others, and thereby reinforcing the beliefs for yourself, that you are unworthy, a failure, unlovable, incapable, clingy, avoidant, detached, guarded, critical, rejecting, approval-seeking, or conflict avoidant. You might be thinking that this doesn't sound like a recipe for a healthy, loving relationship. And you're right! A healthy relationship can't exist without healthy communication.

Let's start by bringing awareness to your unhelpful patterns of communication. As you read, keep in mind that much like your core beliefs, you were doing the best you could to protect yourself as a child when these patterns formed. You might experience feelings of shame, guilt, or regret as you complete these exercises. Let those negative feelings go—they no longer serve you. Focus on celebrating the fact that you are bringing awareness to the core-belief-driven communication patterns and behaviors that are inconsistent with your values.

Unhealthy Communication

There are several communication styles that can create blocks to intimacy. These unhealthy communication styles might be long-established patterns that you've accepted because they're all you've known. Or you might engage in these forms of communication when you're triggered or when you're in a trauma bond.

When you get triggered, you are no longer focused on your values and the big picture. Your focus narrows to the immediate urge to reduce and eliminate the negative thoughts and feelings that have become intolerable. You might find yourself doing or saying things that make the situation worse. In these moments, your intense emotional state has overridden your cognitive state. In other words, your amygdala—the part of your brain that experiences emotions and gets your brain and body to respond when danger arises—has hijacked the part of your brain that guides you to rational action, your prefrontal cortex, keeping you from being able to think rationally.

When your emotions are overpowering your rational mind, it's likely that you'll default to unhelpful patterns of communication and behavior. Your ability to hear what the other person is saying is diminished when your amygdala is in charge. These blocks to listening are also connected to your core beliefs—in that you "hear" what you are expecting to hear and what you've heard in the past. And you're likely reacting in old and familiar ways. Your mind always wants to take shortcuts because they make things easier. Why spend extra time assessing a situation, asking clarifying questions, and coming to a thoughtful conclusion when you can just assume that it's going to be like it's always been? You may as well react the way you've always reacted. After all, it kept you safe. Unfortunately, it comes with a price: trauma bonds and toxic relationships. Your communication patterns are often driven by fear. And sometimes, this fear and the limits you give your own behavior as a result also breed resentment, driving you to lash out in whatever ways you feel you can—even as your toxic relationships continue (Smith 2011).

To begin changing this dynamic, we'll examine the influence of some crucial factors on what we feel and how we communicate it. These are the typical threat responses of our amygdala—fight, flight, freeze, or force—and the typical communication behaviors and styles we can fall into when we haven't been taught how to process our own emotions and instincts.

Fight, Flight, Freeze, or Force

Again, letting others know who we are by expressing our thoughts, preferences, and emotions can feel risky. You likely learned that a safe way to avoid these feelings and be accepted was to please others by agreeing with them. And over time, you've repressed your thoughts and feelings. They might surface occasionally when you're angry or frustrated, but you may be quick to back down when they are met with resistance or anger. Or perhaps you direct your aggression at the people you feel you can while letting problematic dynamics with toxic partners continue.

When your core beliefs are triggered, how do you respond? When you're having a conflict with another person, it's likely that you're reacting automatically with behaviors that are unhelpful in the present. The primitive, emotional part of your brain reacts quickly and automatically to perceived danger. The primitive mind is the part of the mind that's focused solely on survival—that primal instinct that we're born with dominates our early years and activates throughout our lives when we feel threatened. Primitive reactions can be categorized as fight, flight, freeze, or force behaviors (McKay, Lev, and Skeen 2012):

- Aggression or hostility, including blaming, criticizing, challenging, or resisting (fight)

- Demanding, controlling, insisting in an effort to control the situation (fight)

- Manipulation, threats, dishonesty (fight)

- Minimizing the other person's needs (fight)

- Appearing to be compliant but rebelling by complaining or pouting (fight)

- Giving in, complying, avoiding conflict, being passive or submissive, trying to please (freeze)

- Clinging, dependence, attention seeking, reassurance seeking (force)

- Retreating emotionally, physically, sexually (flight)

- Avoiding by seeking excitement and distraction through work, shopping, gambling, sex, risk-taking activities (flight)

- Avoiding by numbing with alcohol, drugs, food, TV, social media (flight)

- Disconnecting and withdrawing from others (flight)

Fight, Flight, Freeze, or Force Behaviors

Which of these behaviors do you most commonly engage in? Take a moment to journal about them now—as well as the elements of your core beliefs you feel might drive you to these behaviors when you're triggered in your trauma-bonded relationships and otherwise.

How does it feel to bring awareness to your communication style? Are you able to connect it to your childhood experiences? Write down your experiences along with thoughts about how you developed this style of interacting with others.

Remember Camila from previous chapters? Here's what she wrote: "Yikes! It's embarrassing to look at my style of communication in these terms. I knew from my nine traits that I was intense, and I knew from my anxious attachment and my abandonment and emotional deprivation core-belief statements that I was clingy, but I never thought of it in terms of 'force.' But I can see that I am trying to force myself on someone else because of my fears. Even more embarrassing and shaming is admitting that I use manipulation and dishonesty in dating and relationships. And I can see that these behaviors aren't working for me, at least not in the long run. Relating them to my childhood experiences, I know that the clinging was with my mom when she wasn't working. When she was home, I was stuck to her like we were glued together. When I think about it now, I feel sad for her that she never had any time for herself. She was either working endless hours or with me. As for the manipulation and dishonesty, I used that with my dad to try to get him to visit me."

Here's what Ian wrote for this exercise: "I take 'flight'—my specialty is disconnecting and withdrawing from others. It's clearly connected to my childhood and my home environment. I think it conditioned me to keep to myself. It's interesting to think about these behaviors as primal or survival behaviors. That feels very accurate to me and my experience. But I'm beginning to understand how these survival behaviors have created obstacles to my happiness and my ability to connect with others."

Now, let's look at what Aryan wrote: "It's clear to me that my primitive reactions haven't changed since I was a kid. I give in, I comply. I avoid conflict at all costs. I'm passive and submissive, and I'm always trying to please my partner because I depend upon him and I don't want him to leave me. All of my behaviors are identified as 'freeze,' and that is exactly how I feel: frozen by fear of being abandoned and all that it represents. This relates so powerfully to my brother's death."

Remember that the part of your mind that drives you to behave this way doesn't have a current or accurate view of the threat you feel you're facing; it's stuck in the past. Identifying these long-standing fear responses might bring up feelings of shame, and it's crucial to meet those feelings with understanding and self-compassion. The purpose of this exercise is to bring awareness to the obstacles that are preventing you from creating healthy communication and relationships. Remember, you are on a path to change.

Also bear in mind that you might not always react the same way. If you're in a relationship trauma bond or a toxic relationship, you might have reacted in different ways based upon how the other person reacted to you. As you continue to consider your communication style and your typical behaviors in your relationships, make a note of your partner's behaviors too. It will be helpful to bring awareness to the dynamic that's at play in your relationship. (If you aren't currently in a relationship, make note of the dynamics in your most recent relationship.)

Typical Communication Obstacles

Now, let's look at some of the other obstacles to healthy communication. Again, these are likely long-standing patterns that are operating outside of your awareness (Skeen 2014).

Mind reading. Mind reading is a block to healthy communication that is driven by the fear associated with your core beliefs. You already assume what the other person is going to say—*They think I'm incompetent; they don't want to be with me; they want to hurt me*—based upon your experiences and core beliefs. You might conclude what's going to happen based upon the presenting emotion of the other person. And if you react "as if" they are saying what you predicted, then you are on a path to a self-fulfilling prophecy.

Filtering. Again, in filtering, the communication is getting distorted because you are hearing only part of what the other person is saying. If your core-belief-driven thoughts are operating outside of awareness, you might hear only the negative, which you will use to reinforce your beliefs—*This means they are going to leave me; this means I'm not good enough; this means no one's ever going to love me*—while ignoring, or filtering out, the positive.

Placating. Placating is a common communication block for someone who is conflict avoidant. This might be relevant for you if you grew up in a household where the expression of anger or other negative emotions came with consequences. You learned to agree, make promises, apologize, or do whatever it took to de-escalate and avoid conflict. This is likely your style if your temperament is passive and avoidant (refer to the "Temperament and Coping Styles" section in chapter 3).

Sparring. In contrast, if you have a more energetic and aggressive temperament, sparring might be one of your blocks to healthy communication. Maybe your style of coping when you felt unsafe during your developmental years was to argue or debate in response to criticism. If so, it makes sense that this is your automatic response to a situation that triggers a heightened emotional reaction.

Judging. If you are quick to judge other people, this tendency can be a protective reaction. As a child, you became hypervigilant in an effort to keep yourself safe. This led you to make snap judgments about your environment and the people in it. This might be an automatic behavior, particularly if you have a mistrust and abuse core belief.

Comparing. Making comparisons might be a block to healthy communication for you if you were compared unfavorably to a sibling or peers or if you felt like any accomplishment was always held up to the accomplishments of others. This may resonate with you if you have failure, defectiveness, or dependence core beliefs.

Now that you've read the blocks to developing healthy communication and relationships, write down the ones that are relevant for you, including any core belief statements that relate to any of the communication styles. You might be experiencing feelings of shame; that is normal when bringing awareness to unpleasant aspects of ourselves. But remember, this is what you learned when you didn't know any better. Now you have the power to change the way that you connect with others. To that end, let's look at healthy communication styles.

Healthy Communication

In *The Art of Communicating*, Thich Nhat Hanh (2013) says communication should be viewed much in the same way we view food. Are we ingesting what is nourishing us, or are we ingesting what is toxic to us? And what are we feeding others? Are we harming each other with toxic words, or are we nourishing each other with words that will help us grow and thrive? This is a helpful way to think about how you're communicating with others and what type of communication you are allowing from others.

Breaking free from the cycle of toxic communication isn't easy. You've likely been hiding and protecting parts of yourself because you fear rejection, that you will be taken advantage of, or that you will be ridiculed. Each of these fears is tied to your core beliefs. It's also possible that you had a traumatic relationship experience that resulted in the inability for you to trust yourself or others. Whatever your experience, it was painful, and you've been behaving and interacting in ways that you hoped would alleviate your pain. Unfortunately, these efforts, while understandable, have kept you stuck in trauma bonds and toxic relationships and prevented you from developing healthy attachments. They've put a barrier between you and the relationships that you deserve.

Let's look at ways of communicating that will enable you to develop authentic connections with nontoxic people—people who are willing to see you for who you are, care for you, love you, and speak to you sincerely and genuinely. We'll cover a number of techniques: skillful self-disclosure, how to deal with others' silence or lack of communication, active listening, and how to set boundaries and stick to them.

Self-Disclosure

Just thinking about what the term "self-disclosure" represents—communicating who you are, how you feel, what matters to you, and what you really want—might make you nervous. This is a normal reaction when you've experienced unpleasant, hurtful, or even painful reactions to sharing parts of yourself with others. It's likely conditioned you to hide the parts of yourself that you were told were unlovable or unacceptable. And it's likely that parts of yourself were hidden from your consciousness. Hopefully, the previous chapters have brought awareness to the core beliefs that have been operating unconsciously. As you know, our beliefs drive automatic behaviors, including communication, which reflects who you are and how others experience you. Increased self-awareness will enable you to communicate more effectively about who you are and what you care about.

Self-disclosure can be challenging. When it's done properly, it's rewarding and enriching for you and your relationships; it can also be a struggle to figure out how to do it well, especially when you're adjusting long-standing patterns of evasion and discomfort. You've probably been on the listening end of a conversation with someone you barely know who "over-shared" about their life, including challenging and painful experiences. It felt like too much too soon. More than likely, they had some regret about sharing such intimate details of their life with someone they didn't know well, and you felt uncomfortable and uncertain about what to do with the information. The motivation for this self-disclosure might be a rush to make a quick connection fueled by the "urge to merge" or a test, as if to say, "Here I am. Can you handle all of this? Can you love someone who has this baggage?" (Salzberg 2018).

It may have even ended the budding relationship because neither of you knew how to navigate the awkwardness. Unfortunately, most early connections can't withstand the weight of too much too soon.

You may have found yourself in a situation where you regretted the amount of information you shared with someone. The following core belief statements might help you bring some awareness to what's driving that tendency.

- *I cling to people because I'm afraid they will leave me.* This statement often reflects an abandonment core belief. You might feel an unconscious pull to get close to someone quickly.

- *I get so obsessed with the idea that my lovers will leave me that I drive them away.* This statement often reflects an abandonment core belief. In this case, you might be sharing too much too soon as a test to see if it will drive them away.

- *I set up tests for people to see if they are really on my side.* Again, this is a test, often prompted by a mistrust and abuse core belief, to determine if the other person can be trusted to stick around and not use your intimate details against you.

- *I am often drawn to people who are critical and reject me.* With this, often driven by a defectiveness core belief, you might be unconsciously providing information about yourself that they can weaponize against you later.

- *I give more to others than they give to me.* This is often the result of a subjugation core belief; when you overshare, you are unconsciously providing more information to reinforce this core belief statement.

- *I really worry about pleasing people and getting their approval.* Again, you are behaving and communicating in line with your subjugation core beliefs.

- *I do not have someone who really listens and is tuned in to my true needs and feelings.* If this statement, often the product of an emotional deprivation core belief, is valid for you, then it feels good to you when someone shows an interest in you and your life. In this situation, you might find yourself sharing more than you intended.

Also, if you have an anxious attachment style, you might share more to rush the connection in an effort to alleviate the anxiety that you experience. Can you identify with any of the above statements? Write down the ones that are relevant for you.

Here's Tayshia's story. She met Ahmed, and they had instant chemistry. In the span of a week, they went on three dates; each was more fun than the last. Tayshia was hopeful that she would finally be able to delete her dating apps and settle into a relationship with a great guy. She had spent the last six months processing being dumped out of the blue by her boyfriend of a year.

So when Ahmed asked her if she wanted to go away for the weekend, she couldn't think of anything she'd rather do. The weekend was filled with outdoor adventures, great food, and dreamy pillow talk. And it seemed like Ahmed wanted to know everything about her. Ahmed would often say, "When you know, you know," in reference to the great connection he was feeling with her. He asked Tayshia lots of questions about herself and her past relationships, specifically the one that had abruptly ended six months ago. It felt good to have someone show such an interest in her on more than a superficial level. He was a great listener. Ahmed didn't go into great detail when Tayshia asked him questions (for example, "I have problems with my brother, but I'll tell you about that another time," "My last relationship ended, but there are no hard feelings"). But she wasn't worried because, as he explained, he just wanted to focus on her. Two weeks later, after postponing their planned dates, he texted her to say that he just wasn't comfortable moving forward with her. His explanation: "I feel like you're still hung up on your last boyfriend."

Tayshia was stunned. Once she worked through the emotional pain, she was able to reflect on the experience and see where her abandonment and emotional deprivation core beliefs had made her vulnerable to disclosing too much too soon. She felt an intensity with Ahmed that made him feel familiar, like she'd known him for longer than she had. And with her core beliefs operating outside of awareness, she was vulnerable to someone who was acting as if they were meeting her needs for connection and understanding.

Was Ahmed a toxic person, or had Tayshia "scared him off" by disclosing too much too soon, even though he asked her the questions about her relationship history? Whatever you answered, you're correct! This is a trick question. Both can be true, and sometimes it can be difficult or impossible to know what was really at play. Ahmed could be a bad actor who was just trying to get Tayshia to sleep with him. Maybe he manipulated her by acting deeply interested in her. It certainly wasn't realistic to think that after one date, he knew she was the one—his words, "When you know, you know." Alternatively, it might be off-putting to someone who isn't comfortable with handling difficult or complicated emotions to hear about a past relationship. Maybe, in this case, Ahmed found himself overwhelmed by what Tayshia had shared. And ultimately, he didn't feel equipped to handle being in a relationship with her.

If you, like Tayshia, have an emotional deprivation core belief and your experience was that you weren't listened to or valued, being on the receiving end of someone who is very interested in you—asking lots of questions—might feel good. However, it could also indicate a lack of balance. Ask yourself the following questions to assess where the two of you are at:

- Are you learning as much about them as they're learning about you?

- Is there mutual self-disclosure?

- What have you learned about the other person?

- What does the other person know about you?

- Is the other person asking all the questions?

- How are they responding when you ask them a question? Are they vague or forthcoming?

Also, keep in mind the number of dates and the amount of time you've spent together. If you keep track of your dates in your journal, it's less likely that you'll share too much too soon. Also, make every effort to engage in self-disclosure in person. It's important that both of you are able to take in all the obvious and subtle ways that you each communicate verbally and nonverbally. It will give you the opportunity to notice if the other person is uncomfortable with what you are telling them or if they are fully engaged. Take note of facial expressions, body language, eye contact, subtle noises, gestures, and if their words are aligned with their nonverbal forms of communication. You lose the ability to capture that information if your communications happen over text or direct message.

Now let's look at core belief statements that might indicate your tendency to withhold information about yourself. When you're unable to open up about yourself, it makes it difficult for the other person to connect with you. It can often be interpreted as a lack of interest on your part or a feeling that you have something to hide. Either way, it's a missed opportunity for connection.

- *I expect people to hurt me or use me.* This is the product of a mistrust and abuse core belief.

- *I have to protect myself and stay on my guard.* This statement reflects a mistrust and abuse core belief.

- *If I'm not careful, people will take advantage of me.* This concern illustrates a mistrust and abuse core belief.

- *I am afraid to let people get close to me because I expect them to hurt me.* This fear is a result of a mistrust and abuse core belief.

- *No one really understands me.* This is a product of an emotional deprivation core belief.

- *It is hard for me to let people love me.* This is also a product of an emotional deprivation core belief.

- *No person could love me if they really knew me.* This is a result of a defectiveness core belief.

- *I have secrets that I don't want to share, even with the people closest to me.* This is a product of a defectiveness core belief.

- *One of my greatest fears is that my faults will be exposed.* This fear is a result of a defectiveness core belief.

- *I feel embarrassed around other people because I do not measure up in terms of my accomplishments.* This is a product of a failure core belief.

Ideally, you pace the self-disclosure. If you've been hiding parts of yourself or rushing to overshare, it can be challenging to know how to strike the right balance. While on this path to healing, you've gained some additional understanding and awareness about yourself. And with that, you've been able to process and release the shame that may have been holding you back from sharing parts of yourself. If you've been in a relationship trauma bond or you're currently in one, you've likely experienced the pain of someone you trusted and loved weaponizing your vulnerabilities. So you may be reluctant to share parts of yourself. That reluctance is valid and highlights why it's important to pace yourself so you get to know the person before you share information that would allow a toxic person to take advantage of you.

Silence

Technology has increased our expectation to receive an immediate response from others and diminished our ability to sit with the silence that exists in the absence of a response. This is even more challenging for people with an abandonment, mistrust and abuse, emotional deprivation, or defectiveness core belief. It's likely that your worst fears get triggered when the person doesn't respond to your text right away. Your mind can quickly fill in the void with fear-based thoughts: *They don't like me. They're with someone else. They met someone better than me. What if something has happened to them?* Sitting with uncertainty can feel intolerable. When you can't endure the pain anymore, you reach out again. Depending upon your communication style, you might text something like:

- "Are you alive?" which is sarcastic and passive aggressive.

- "Why aren't you responding?" This is direct and aggressive.

- "Hey, just checking in again. I hope you're okay," a more passive communication style.

It's also important to look at your past experience with silence. It's likely that your foundational relationships are causing you to distort your present reality (Rosenberg 2015). In your journal, write down what silence means to you, how it connects to your childhood experiences, and how you react to silence. Does it represent:

- Loss?

- Rejection?

- Punishment?

- Control or manipulation?

Remember Amber from chapter 5? Let's see what she wrote about her experience with silence: "Silence is pure torture for me. My mind fills the void with fear-based thoughts like: *Did I do something wrong? Are they mad at me? They're ignoring me because they saw me for who I really am, a deeply flawed person.* I didn't realize until now that it's tied to my mother. When my mother was upset, she would withdraw. My brothers didn't care, they didn't bother trying to find out what was wrong, and from what I could tell, my dad didn't make any effort to cheer her up or resolve the problem. I, on the other hand, tried everything to get her to engage with me. And, now that I think about it, I never even entertained the thought that her upset could be unrelated to me. As an adult, looking back, I recognize that it probably had everything to do with my dad (her husband). But I was the one who tried to make her feel better because I assumed I was the problem and I needed to fix it. I was accommodating and helpful—I would do anything to get her to engage with me. So I feel like I associate silence with loss, rejection, punishment, control, and manipulation. As an adult, I interpret silence as anger, disappointment, disapproval, or unhappiness with me. In the absence of a timely (and my judgment about time is likely distorted) response, I often text, "Are you mad at me?" The reply I receive 90 percent of the time is, "Why would I be mad at you?" I know that it has pushed people away from me, and I can see that in situations where I'm truly being neglected or ignored, I've accepted it because it's familiar to me. My current partner shuts down when he's upset with me. And I have a pattern of accommodating him to get him to reengage with me. Even if it means apologizing or accepting the blame for our conflict when it wasn't my fault. I can see now why it's a pattern with us. We never resolve issues or come to a mutual understanding through conversation because I'm so relieved when he's speaking to me again."

How do you feel after bringing awareness to your relationship with silence? Do you find yourself stuck in a pattern that relates to relationships from your childhood? As you bring awareness to your unconscious thoughts and behaviors, are you able to recognize how they might be out of alignment with your present-day experience? In the next chapter, using mindfulness will help you sit with the discomfort of silence.

Now, let's look at some tools that can assist you in overcoming some of the blocks to listening.

Active Listening

Earlier you identified your blocks to listening (mind reading, filtering, placating, sparring, judging, and comparing). Now, we're going to look at an effective way to engage in a conversation: active listening. Active listening is an integral skill for healthy communication that necessitates staying engaged with your conversation partner and bringing awareness to your blocks to listening throughout the conversation. The process of active listening involves three steps:

1. Paraphrasing

2. Clarifying

3. Providing feedback

Paraphrasing involves repeating what your conversation partner said to you in your own words. You might start off with, "What I'm hearing is..." or "I understand that you..." Paraphrasing clears up any miscommunications or misunderstandings. Paraphrasing also helps you avoid listening blocks because you have to pay close attention to the content of what they're saying as they're saying it. You'll also have an easier time remembering what your conversation partner said because you repeated it back to them. Another benefit of paraphrasing is that it makes your conversation partner feel truly heard and potentially validated.

Clarifying builds upon paraphrasing. Clarifying involves asking questions to confirm you've understood correctly or to clear up any misunderstandings between the two of you. You can lead with, "To check my understanding, you've said..." or "When you said _____, what did you mean by that?" Your conversation partner also has the opportunity to expand on anything they've said, especially when you feel you need more information to fully comprehend. Another benefit of clarifying is that it demonstrates to your conversation partner that you genuinely want to understand them and their perspective.

The final step in the process of active listening is providing feedback. At this point in the conversation, it's your turn to share your thoughts and feelings in response to what your conversation partner has told you. Because you've paraphrased their statements and clarified any misunderstandings, you should have an accurate understanding of their perspective. When providing feedback, follow these three principles: do so immediately, lead with honesty, and be supportive. It's important that you provide your feedback in the moment, when their perspective is fresh in your mind. Also, this will avoid your conversation partner feeling like you're hiding something from them. And when you pair honesty with support, you ensure that your message is true and kind (McKay, Davis, and Fanning 2009).

Setting Boundaries

Setting boundaries might be one of the most challenging communication skills to adopt if you:

- Fear rejection that's associated with an abandonment core belief

- Worry what others will think of you, which is a prevalent thought with a defectiveness core belief

- Feel that the needs of others are more important than your own, which is a hallmark of a subjugation core belief

- Fear that the other person will stop giving you the love you desire, which is a prevalent concern with an emotional deprivation core belief

- Rely on the other person and have a dependence core belief

- Don't trust others to respect your boundaries, which is common with a mistrust or abuse core belief

- Feel like you won't be able to enforce your boundaries, which is common concern associated with a failure core belief.

There can be many obstacles in your mind that might prevent you from setting boundaries to protect yourself from toxic behavior and people. But boundaries are an important part of healthy relationships. Setting boundaries will likely feel uncomfortable and awkward at first, but with practice, you will appreciate their value, and you will get more comfortable.

Here are six steps to setting boundaries:

1. Bring awareness to your priorities and values. What matters to you? Refer to your list of values.

2. Communicate with clarity. Clear statements might include, "Please don't _____." Speaking with clarity means that the other person will understand what you're saying. Write down your boundary statements and practice them so you're prepared when the time comes.

3. Be prepared to experience discomfort when communicating your boundaries. Stay present and grounded in your values to get through the discomfort.

4. Be ready for pushback. This won't happen all the time, but you will have people who won't respect your boundaries for various reasons.

5. Identify the consequences for someone who isn't respecting your boundaries. For example, "If you continue to speak to me this way, our date is over."

6. Make sure you are respecting other people's boundaries.

Again, this is a necessary and positive aspect of a healthy relationship.

Moving Forward

In the next chapter, you'll learn the importance of mindfulness. It's particularly helpful when you are triggered by an event and faced with the choice of relying on your fear-driven coping behaviors or choosing your new value-driven intention.

CHAPTER 8

Staying Present with Mindfulness

In the previous chapters, you brought awareness to your core beliefs and their origins, as well as the thoughts and behaviors associated with your beliefs. You were able to make sense of how your behaviors developed. And now you likely have a better understanding of how your mind is designed for safety and survival. It's meant to help you, but sometimes it overreacts like a helicopter parent—hypervigilant, overprotective, and intrusive but well-meaning. When this happens, the thoughts, emotions, and bodily sensations generated by the mind can drive you to behave in ways that cause more discomfort by creating additional problems. The overprotective, overreactive mind can push you, if you allow it, to behave in ways that take you away from your stated values.

Again, this part of your mind is perceiving a threat. When that perception goes unchecked, you default to your automatic reactions. When you were a child, this tendency helped you: you were in situations that scared you, and your mind guided you to react in the ways you felt would help you survive. But you're not a child anymore; you don't need to behave in the same ways to stay safe. Your automatic and habitual behaviors are no longer helpful in your current environment. In fact, they are harmful to you and your relationships. They are creating unnecessary pain. You can choose to opt out of this secondary pain with mindfulness.

Mindfulness can change this unhelpful cycle by bringing awareness to the moment-by-moment experience. Your automatic reactions have gained strength over time, so it won't be easy to break the patterns, but you have some helpers: your values. You are going to be guided by your values to make a shift from primitive reaction to meaningful action. Let's look at how a mindfulness practice can positively impact your relationship with yourself and others.

Benefits of Mindfulness

Before we get into the specifics of a mindfulness practice, let's look at some of the benefits of mindfulness. This should serve as motivation for incorporating mindfulness into your daily life.

- Mindfulness enhances your awareness of daily life, which increases your feelings of well-being.

- Mindfulness increases psychological flexibility, which allows you to acknowledge that unpleasant and intolerable thoughts can exist without your having to act on them and that you can instead make the choice to act on your values.

- Mindfulness enables you to bring attention to your values and act in line with them.

- Mindfulness promotes emotion regulation by allowing your emotions to exist without reacting automatically and unconsciously to them.

- Mindfulness engages you in self-compassion—being kind and understanding to yourself rather than judgmental and critical. It provides you with the ability to acknowledge that mistakes are part of being human (Davis and Hayes 2011). And it provides you with distance from your behaviors (*I did something bad, but I am not bad*).

- A regular mindfulness practice has been shown to decrease the gray matter in the brain's amygdala region (the seat of our emotions) and increase it in several parts of the brain that are involved in learning, memory, and emotion regulation (Yang et al. 2019).

These are compelling reasons to adopt a regular mindfulness practice. Mindfulness will help you tolerate the intense negative emotions that you experience when your core beliefs get triggered. By tolerating these emotions and not acting on them, you can end the dysfunctional cycle that your fear-based behaviors perpetuate. When you are in the present moment, not gripped by the pain of the past or panicked about the possibilities in the future, you can more easily regulate your emotions and engage in the communication and behavior that lead to healthy attachments. With practice, you will recognize when your fear-driven core beliefs get triggered, pay attention in a nonjudgmental way to your inner experience, tolerate the overwhelming emotions, and respond in a value-driven way (Harris 2021a).

Observing Your Thoughts

We tend to accept our thoughts as facts. This is especially true if your thoughts are core-belief-driven:

- *Everyone I love leaves me.* This thought is the result of an abandonment core belief.

- *I have to protect myself so others won't hurt me.* This is the product of a mistrust and abuse core belief.

- *I'll never get the love I need.* This thought is the result of an emotional deprivation core belief.

- *I am unworthy of love.* This is the product of a defectiveness core belief.

- *I'm a failure.* This thought is the result of a failure core belief.

- *I'm not capable.* This is the product of a dependence core belief.

- *The needs of others matter more than mine.* This thought is the result of a subjugation core belief.

It's likely that you have come to believe, consciously or unconsciously, in statements related to your core beliefs. Core beliefs and their associated statements can feel like they are as much a part of you as your eye color. A regular mindfulness practice can help you detach from your negative beliefs and thoughts (van Vreeswijk, Broersen, and Schurink 2014).

The problem with treating our thoughts as facts is that we often unconsciously behave in ways that reinforce these thoughts, thereby turning them into reality. By learning to accept your thoughts without judgment, criticism, or trying to change them, you can create distance between you and your thoughts. As meditation teacher Jon Kabat-Zinn says, a thought is not a fact—a thought is just a thought.

Beginning Mindfulness Exercise: Observing Your Mind

You may find this exercise challenging in the beginning because you are going to aim to be nonjudgmental. After a lifetime of judging yourself, it's going to be difficult to break this habit. But with practice, you will. Be patient with yourself.

This exercise will take five minutes. Set a timer (if you're using your smartphone, put it on the "Do not disturb" setting). Sit comfortably in a chair, or if it's easier for you, lie down. Close your eyes. Bring your attention to your thoughts. When a thought enters your mind, notice it without judging, criticizing, or trying to change it. You'll notice that the thoughts keep coming like leaves floating down a stream, clouds moving across the sky, or luggage on an airport carousel. You might be having the thought that it's difficult to hang onto a thought. Thoughts come and go. You might find yourself slipping into judgments of liking some thoughts or wanting to push away unpleasant thoughts. Just keep bringing your attention back to observing your thoughts without judgment.

Doing this mindfulness exercise on a daily basis, ideally in the morning, will help you detach from your core-belief-related thoughts. Start with five minutes and build up to ten minutes. After you finish your morning practice, see if you can take the attention, openness, and acceptance of the experience into your day.

Do the Opposite

If you're like most people who have been reacting in a mindless way versus responding in a mindful way, you noticed a big contrast between the two. You might even say that they're opposites. In fact, "do the opposite" is a helpful strategy.

The most memorable example of "do the opposite" is from a *Seinfeld* episode. Jerry, George, and Elaine are at their usual diner, engaged in conversation, when George tells them that every decision he's made in his entire life has been wrong. His life is the complete opposite of everything he wanted it to be. He doesn't have a job, he's broke, he's living with his parents, and he doesn't have a girlfriend. In response, Jerry advises him to do the opposite. He tells him that if every instinct he has is wrong, then the opposite of every instinct would have to be right. It's a humorous exchange that results in some successes for George when he implements Jerry's advice.

Like George, we all get stuck in patterns that no longer serve us. And usually, they are operating outside of awareness to the extent that they just feel like part of us. Recognizing our reactions and choices can be powerful. And this is especially so when you're in a relationship trauma bond and you feel like you don't have control or you're out of control. This is an opportunity to take control and make a choice (often it will be the opposite of your default reaction) to align with your values.

When you move from the primitive reaction to the meaningful action, you are departing from what is known and familiar—what feels safe—and you are stepping into the unknown, being asked to embrace uncertainty— what feels unsafe to the part of you that reacts automatically. Your fear-driven thoughts will remind you that it's safer to stay in the behavioral loop that's helped to keep you safe your entire life. It's a compelling argument. But you're here, reading this book because you want a different life. You want to take charge of what you can control and come to terms with what you can't control. With effort and practice, you can learn to regulate your behavior by bringing awareness to the present moment, you can recognize what your primitive mind is trying to make you do, and instead, you can engage the rational mind and choose a meaningful action.

The transition from core-belief-driven behavior to value-driven behavior will not be easy. But your path to this point has not been easy—in fact, it's been painful and disappointing at times. And with every meaningful action you successfully take, your rational mind will become stronger, and every time you ignore your primitive mind's reaction, it will lose strength. It won't happen overnight, but with mastery of two factors—time and mindfulness—it will happen.

Exercise: Determining Valued Actions

Take out your journal and refer to your notes from chapter 6. Select your top five values. Next to each value, write the current behaviors that are taking you further away from your stated value. Then, write down the behavior that is aligned with your value.

Value:

Instinctive reaction:

Meaningful action:

Remember Joy from previous chapters? Let's see how she filled out this exercise:

Value: *Gratitude*

Instinctive reaction: *If I find myself disappointed or upset about something, I focus on the negative. It's like I can't see the forest for the trees. Once I start down a negative path, it feels like there's no going back. I shut down: I can't acknowledge what's good, and I can't reciprocate good feelings from others, such as my friends.*

Meaningful action: *I consciously step back from the negative path I'm headed down, and I return the kindness and appreciation that my friends give to me. Engaging in a gratitude practice reminds me that there is good in my life.*

Value: *Self-respect*

Instinctive reaction: *Even when I know I'm being mistreated by the person I'm dating or a family member, I'll often excuse the behavior because I don't want them to leave me. This makes me feel even worse about myself and like I deserve to be mistreated. This instinctive reaction is definitely related to my problem of misreading intensity as intimacy. Intensity can take the form of bad behavior that I'll excuse because it makes me think they really want me.*

Meaningful action: *I set a firm boundary with the person I'm dating when they're not treating me the way I need and deserve to be treated. I communicate my needs clearly.*

Value: *Belonging*

Instinctive reaction: *When I'm not immediately accepted by someone I'm dating or a new friend, I want to stop putting in effort. When I don't feel welcomed right away, it feels like I'll never really belong.*

Meaningful action: *Even when faced with initial uncertainty about my connection with someone, like a new friend, I put forth the effort and see if I'm met with that same effort and interest.*

Value: *Closeness*

Instinctive reaction: *When I feel like I'm being rejected, I shut down and don't show that person how much I want them to want me and how much I want them.*

Meaningful action: *If I want intimacy and connection in my life, I have to be brave enough to show that I care.*

Value: *Dependability*

Instinctive reaction: *Because my dad abandoned my family, I'm often expecting that other people in my life will leave too. Like I said before, when somebody seems like they may be pulling away, I take it as a sign that they don't care about me and won't ever be there for me.*

Meaningful action: *I want people I can depend and rely on. When I feel insecure or anxious about whether or not I can depend on a trusted person, I should tell them about my concerns and explain to them what I need to see in order to feel more at ease.*

Read over your responses. What do you notice as you look at your instinctive reaction and your meaningful action? Are you struck by the contrast between the two?

Here's what Joy shared: *The contrast between my instinctive reaction and meaningful action is night and day. One thing I notice for each value is that maybe if I just stepped back, calmed down, and considered the situation more holistically, I could get to that meaningful action.*

Eventually, you should do this exercise with all your values, as a way of giving yourself a map for a life in which you truly *live* all these values, rather than living the way fear and trauma bonding may have conditioned you to do.

One Valued Action

Over the next week, choose at least one of the valued actions you outlined and do it. Then, journal about the experience. It doesn't matter how big or small the action is; any action is worth doing and reflecting on. What was it like to behave in a way that runs counter to what trauma bonds have guided you to do for so long? Was it scary? Was it freeing? Was it a little of both?

If you like, repeat this exercise for other valued actions you've written down.

Time

Our primitive mind—designed as it was to help us thrive in a much more dangerous human past—wants us to act quickly (fight, flight, freeze, or force). There's no time to think; if you hesitate, you might be killed. This makes time itself a useful tool for transitioning from the highly emotional reaction that accompanies a triggering event. The anxiety, the feeling in the pit of your stomach, and the racing thoughts you experience will lose their power if you give them time. Time will give you the opportunity to shift your focus from the past to the present. When your mind is focused on the present, you can become the curious observer of your experience. When you arrive at the present moment, the negative emotions, thoughts, and sensations that are rooted in the past will lose their power, and the primitive mind will become less compelling. You will be able to choose a valued action.

When you are triggered, it can feel like you need to act immediately—it feels urgent. In most situations, it's rarely an emergency. Your primitive mind is trying to keep you safe, so it will always make you feel like you need to act quickly. Bring awareness to what is time sensitive, what is urgent, and what is important.

There are some useful tools that you can utilize to assist you in getting through an emotional storm following a triggering event to a calm place where you can make values-driven choices. Let's explore two key tools together: journaling and spending time in nature.

Journaling

You've already been using the first tool we recommend for getting through your emotional storm: journaling, the act of writing down your thoughts and feelings. One reason we incorporate journal exercises in the book is to help you begin to cultivate journaling as a practice that we hope you continue on your path of healing. The act of writing down what you think and feel, as opposed to just thinking or talking about it, can be uniquely beneficial. It can help you learn to hone your attention on the specifics of situations and on the particulars of your own experience—which can be hard to do in the rush of everyday life. Journaling about meaningful topics in your life has also been proven to improve mental health as well as physical well-being. Journaling reduces anxiety, breaks the cycle of obsessive thinking, improves awareness and perception of events, regulates emotions, and improves overall mood. And any reflective practice, like journaling, will help you connect with your values and, as a result, better position you to make values-driven choices.

In the midst of an emotional storm, it can be helpful to pause from whatever you're doing, or whatever situation you find yourself in, and find some private time and space to write and reflect on it. When your fears get triggered and you experience feelings of anxiety, let some of it go on the page. Taking a break to reflect through writing can give you a clearer view of everything. When you sit down to journal, with prompts or exercises like you've found in this book to guide you, or just to write freely, you bring awareness to what you're thinking, feeling, and experiencing in that moment (Nhat Hanh 2012).

Cultivating a journaling practice may seem daunting. Sometimes journaling can bring up very challenging and triggering feelings. Sometimes you might feel self-conscious—the fear of seeing your thoughts and feelings on paper could hold you back from writing them down. Let's talk about a few techniques that might help you get started.

One technique you can use is to start small. Remember Tayshia from chapter 7? She had never kept a journal, and she was nervous about putting her thoughts and feelings on paper. The idea of having to see them written down overwhelmed her. For Tayshia, who tended to hide parts of herself, journaling felt vulnerable. She wanted to start with an accessible approach: bullet journaling. Rather than writing paragraphs about how she was feeling, she jotted down short statements, one at a time. Journaling was a helpful intervention for Tayshia, who struggles with seeing herself and others accurately because of her experience with relationship trauma bonds. If you're also a beginner to journaling like Tayshia, consider starting simple with single statements or questions. Then, you can build up to writing more over time.

Another technique to help you cultivate a journaling practice is to be consistent. You might consider building journaling time into your existing routines. By being consistent and journaling daily or weekly, the practice will become easier for you. When you're journaling consistently, you'll more readily experience the benefits.

The questions and assessments you've answered through reading this book—which have guided you to consider your core beliefs and how they shape your behavior, explore patterns in your life you wish to change, reflect on dates you've gone on and other experiences you have that challenge you, and so on—make for a great start for your journaling practice. Keep going, even if it's just a sentence or a line at a time. Once you've cultivated a regular practice, you'll instinctively turn to your journal following a triggering event. Journaling will help you get in touch with your rational mind and return to a calm place. And of course, your journal can also be a place where you write about your successes—the times you've behaved as your rational mind or your values would have you behave and the positive outcomes and joys doing so made possible.

Spending Time in Nature

Another tool to navigate your emotional storm is to get outdoors and connect with nature. While psychologists long touted the benefits of spending time outside, an evolving body of research suggests that being outside, in a natural environment, like a park or a hiking trail, can indeed have a positive impact on your mental health. When you remove yourself from your typical environment, which is likely to be inside, in your home, you interrupt your automatic behaviors. Getting outside can function as a pause between the triggering person or situation and your resulting emotions. You focus on your new surroundings and ground yourself in the present, moving away from a primitive-mind reaction and toward a rational reaction.

What would it look like to go out for a walk the next time you need to restore calmness? Step outside. Choose a street or road you don't usually walk—avoid the route you routinely take to your bus or subway stop, in your car or on your bike, or to your favorite stores. What or who do you notice as you look around? Name ten things that you observe. Look for a bright color, maybe it's a flower, a front door, or a car. Now look for a pattern. As you direct your attention away from the situation causing you stress, notice if there's a dampening of your negative thoughts and feelings. Continue to make observations about your surroundings: How does the sidewalk feel underneath you? What is the air like today? How does the temperature make you feel? If you cross to the sunny side of the street, does the warmth have any impact on your mood? When you're focused on where your attention goes, and redirecting it if necessary, your mind can be liberated from the trap of the emotional storm.

Now, let's imagine how you might integrate mindfulness into a nature walk or hike. As you navigate the path, do you notice any changes in the landscape? If you didn't know what season it was, would you be able to tell from looking at the trees? Bring awareness to your breath. It may quicken as you reach an incline, and it may slow as you pause your movement to look at an intriguing plant or identify an animal track. When your body is ready for a break, find a place to stop where you won't be interrupted. Take several deep breaths, bringing your body to a resting state. Deep breaths can help restore calmness and relieve stress. Now that you're stopped, bring awareness to other senses. Do you taste anything in particular? Perhaps your mouth feels dry from the physical exertion. What do you smell? The scents may be different if you're seated because your body is closer to the ground. What do you hear? Listen carefully to what's happening around you. What noise stands out to you right away? As you continue listening, what quieter sounds emerge from the background? Grab the dirt, rocks, grass, or other natural material around you with your hand. What is the texture like? How does it feel as you move it between your fingers? When you've finished this sensory exploration, continue down the path. When you finish your walk or hike, think of one word you'd use to describe the environment you navigated. Next, think of a word you'd use to describe how you felt during your emotional storm and a word you'd use to describe how you feel after your experience in nature.

Can a change in environment lead to a change in perspective? Taking a walk with mindfulness as your guide can help promote psychological flexibility and emotion regulation. This activity may not always restore calmness, and it's okay if you only feel that calmness for just a few seconds or minutes. Mindfulness in nature is just one of the many tools you can use to navigate the challenges posed by your experience with relationship trauma bonds and toxic people (Bratman et al. 2019).

Moving Forward

When you have a traumatic experience, the primitive brain generates physical sensations in response to a triggering event: increased heart rate, nausea, panic, and tightness in the chest. You've brought awareness to how your trauma, related fears, and core beliefs are keeping you stuck. And it's likely that you have a better understanding of the changes you can make—value-driven action—to break free of your relationship trauma bonds and toxic people.

However, you will continue to get triggered by a type of person or situation related to your trauma. Your primitive brain will still generate the emotions, thoughts, and sensations that accompany your fears. So that won't change much, but what will change, in a potentially dramatic way, is how you respond to the discomfort. The rational brain can help you resist, with the help of mindfulness, the pull of the primitive brain.

In the next chapter, we will address the grief and loss that accompany the end of even the most toxic relationships.

CHAPTER 9

Acknowledging Grief and Loss

Your life has been filled with loss—what your childhood should have been, the unconditional love you should have experienced, the safety you deserved, the acceptance you longed for, and the guidance you needed. Through the process of identifying your core beliefs and the experiences that formed them, you have brought awareness to the fear-based beliefs that have been driving your choices as well as the healthy experiences that were absent from your formative years. There is a tremendous amount of unacknowledged sadness packed into those years. This chapter is designed to guide you through your feelings of loss and grief. It's likely that you've been engaging in behaviors in an unconscious effort to avoid the powerful emotions associated with loss and grief. You might be afraid to acknowledge your pain because it might feel overwhelming or you fear you might get stuck in the sadness. These fears are understandable. But it's important that you acknowledge your feelings. With your acknowledgment, they will lose the power to control you. It's time to stop avoiding or running away from them.

The trauma of loss is painful. You've already suffered experiences of loss in your life. While it's impossible to identify what type of loss is the most painful, the end of a relationship is incredibly challenging to navigate. And the end of a relationship trauma bond is complicated. Chapter 5, about the tension between intensity and intimacy, highlighted the addictive qualities inherent in a trauma bond—the intensity is unique. As a result, you might experience more intense emotions as you process your loss.

While it's important that you acknowledge your grief from the past, you might also be dealing with the loss of a relationship. The end of a relationship trauma bond or a toxic relationship is painful, even when you know it means progress.

Stages of Grief

We all grieve differently, and healing is rarely linear. Still, Elizabeth Kübler-Ross's five stages of grief offer a useful framework for normalizing your experience. While her theory was originally developed for the death of a loved one, it has been effectively used to frame any loss, including the loss of a relationship. The five stages are denial, bargaining, anger, depression, and acceptance (Harris 2021b).

Denial is a period, often in the beginning, when the loss doesn't feel real. You might experience a sense of numbness or disconnectedness. You might want to avoid talking about it because that will make it feel more real.

Anger is a stage that you will likely go through more than once. If you ended the relationship, your decision to do so might have been accompanied by anger. Maybe they did something that was the final straw for you and you were unwilling to continue to accept their poor treatment of you. Or, post-breakup, as you reflect on the relationship, you may become angry with yourself for what you tolerated from them or how you behaved in response. It's normal that you would experience this emotion as part of the grieving process.

Bargaining is a stage that you might enter as you reflect on the relationship and fantasize about what could have been, what you could have controlled, what you would have done differently if only… You will likely enter this stage as you struggle to come to terms with the future that you'd hoped for during the honeymoon period of the relationship.

Depression refers not to the clinical diagnosis of depression but to the sadness and longing that can accompany the end of your relationship and of your dreams for a happy ending with your person. These feelings will come in waves, and at times they will be unexpected.

Acceptance will come as the pain subsides and you begin to see what is in your control. You will have feelings of hope that you'll have another relationship in the future—one that is healthy and loving. Again, you might cycle through this stage several times until you make peace with your reality.

There is no prescribed order for these stages, and you may not experience all of them, or you might cycle through some of them several times. Ultimately, you'll likely experience many emotions when you make a big transition from what is familiar—even if what's familiar is toxic—to the unknown and uncertainty that accompanies loss (Harris 2021b).

Initially, you might be focused on the horrible things they've done. This might be accompanied by a feeling of relief that you're finally free of them. After those negative thoughts and emotions have lost their power, they might be replaced by thoughts of the good times. That leads to a longing to be with them again. This is often triggered by a date with someone new who you lacked the same chemistry with. And it's likely that you will grieve the loss of your future with that person—the dream that you believed in at the beginning of your relationship when you knew they were "the one."

The primitive brain generates emotions that accompany each of the fear responses: fight, flight, freeze, and force. The fight response will present as anger, frustration, and irritability; the flight response emotions will be fear, anxiety, and worry; the freeze emotional response will present as numbness, apathy, tiredness, zoning out, and disengaging; the force response will present as clinging, dependence, attention seeking, and reassurance seeking. Bring awareness to the emotions that come up for you as you go through the experience of loss. You will also have behaviors associated with your emotional reactions. They can range from isolating and numbing out to distracting yourself, but these almost always create additional issues—compromising your health due to overeating; spending that breaks the budget; drinking or drug use that adds to depression and low self-worth; hooking up, which increases feelings of longing; or reaching out to your ex, which results in regret. Based on your past experiences and your responses to the temperament assessment, can you identify your likely coping behaviors? Can you bring them to awareness so you can avoid them and choose more helpful coping behaviors?

Stages of Grief

Take out your journal and respond to the following prompts. Consider which stage of grief you're currently in, as it relates to your most recent experience with relationship trauma bonds. Which of the stages that we've just covered—denial, bargaining, anger, depression, and acceptance—speak to you? Why? Which of the stages don't speak to you? Why? Thinking about these stages, and the complicated feelings associated with them, may be difficult for you. Take care as you reflect on where you are in the grieving process.

Self-Compassion

You might blame yourself for your relationship experiences, starting in your early childhood and adolescence. Many of the core-belief-driven thoughts cast blame on the child (*It's my fault I wasn't loveable. If only I hadn't been so needy. I needed more love than they could give.*), and this continues into adulthood. It makes sense that you've been stuck in a pattern of acting and reacting to these core beliefs. Practicing self-compassion can help you break free from the behavioral and relationship patterns.

Your inner critic is probably a constant companion with a loud voice. It's distracting, and it's not in the habit of making you feel better about yourself. This is a huge obstacle when you're trying to make positive changes in your life. It's time to replace the inner critic with self-compassion. Maybe you aren't acquainted with self-compassion, but you probably know its sibling, compassion. It's likely that you've provided many people with compassion over the years when they've experienced losses and challenges. You've listened with an open heart and provided words of encouragement and support. Now, it's time for you to turn that compassion toward yourself. It's going to feel uncomfortable and unfamiliar, but it's the inner critic's kryptonite. Our goal is to get rid of your current constant companion because it increases anxiety and depression. Self-compassion decreases anxiety and depression. So, what is self-compassion? Practicing self-compassion involves acknowledging your mistakes and forgiving yourself. It's recognizing when you are suffering and meeting that suffering with kindness (Harvard Health Publishing 2022).

Throughout this book you've brought awareness to what was out of your control: the trauma you experienced as a child, your attachment style, your temperament, and the core beliefs that formed. It's important to acknowledge the loss of the childhood you wish you'd had and the healthy relationships with caregivers, peers, and others that you missed out on. It's often easier to start a self-compassion practice with the child that you once were because it can be difficult to soften your heart for yourself as an adult. It's much easier to practice on the wounded child who is still part of you. To help you access the wounded child in you, try the following self-compassion exercise, which is adapted and modified from *Love Me, Don't Leave Me* (Skeen 2014).

Compassion for Your Childhood Self

Find a photograph of yourself as a child.

Look at the photograph. In your journal, write down what you would do and say to make the child in the photograph feel safe, loved, accepted, appreciated, comforted, valued, adored, and respected.

When you looked at the photograph of yourself, how did it make you feel?

Write down what you would say to that child when they were experiencing the traumatic events that formed their core beliefs.

Use your journal to express your grief about the losses you experienced and the things that were missing in your childhood. Acknowledge the range of emotions that emerge (sadness, anger, regret, guilt, and more) as you allow yourself to grieve.

Were you able to open your heart to yourself?

Did you find it more difficult to be critical of yourself?

Access the photograph and repeat this exercise when you are experiencing negative thoughts and feelings about yourself. Quieting your inner critic and softening your heart will help you heal. Identify a few comforting or reassuring phrases that you can use as a heart opener when your inner critic is present.

Here are some additional ways you can practice self-compassion:

- Do something that makes you feel better physically, such as eating something nutritious; getting a massage, pedicure, or foot massage; taking a yoga class, or going for a walk.

- Talk to yourself like you were talking to a friend. As you go through this period of grieving, imagine what you would say to a friend and say it to yourself. Remember, you are responding to your suffering with kindness.

- Write a letter to yourself. Describe your current situation and be sure to acknowledge your feelings without blaming yourself or anyone else.

- Practice mindfulness. That means observing your thoughts, feelings, and behaviors without judgment. For mindfulness practices, refer to chapter 8 and the next section.

Self-compassion is an unfamiliar and uncomfortable practice after spending a lifetime with the inner critic, but with practice, you will see the benefits of treating yourself with an open heart and mind.

Mindfulness and Grieving

Do you find yourself resisting the complex emotions that you're experiencing following the end of your relationship? Are you struggling to gain control, to be stronger than the unwelcome emotions that can feel overwhelming? As we discussed in chapter 8, mindfulness can help you get to a place where you are able to acknowledge the negative thoughts and feelings as temporary experiences. You might be feeling exhausted from struggling and resisting these thoughts and emotions. What if you stopped the struggle and viewed them as the temporary experiences that they are? The following exercise, which is adapted from *The Interpersonal Problems Workbook* (McKay et al. 2013), will help you observe your negative thoughts and emotions without resisting or struggling to get rid of them.

Mindful Focusing

Consider recording yourself reading the following mindful-focusing practice on your voice memo app. If it's too distracting to hear your own voice, ask a friend or other loved one who you find calming to record it for you.

Close your eyes and take a deep breath…notice the experience of breathing. Observe the feeling of coolness as the breath passes the back of your nose or down the back of your throat. Notice the sensation of your ribs expanding, the air entering your lungs. Be aware of your diaphragm stretching with the breath and the feeling of release as you exhale.

Just keep watching your breath, letting your attention move along the path of flowing air...in and out...in and out. As you breathe, you will also notice other experiences. You may be aware of thoughts: When a thought comes up, say to yourself, *Thought*. Just label it for what it is: thought. And if you're aware of a sensation, whatever it is, say to yourself, *Sensation*. And when you notice an emotion, say to yourself, *Emotion*. Just label it for what it is: emotion.

Try not to hold on to any experience. Just label it and let it go. And wait for the next experience. You are just watching your mind and body, labeling thoughts, sensations, and emotions. If something feels painful, note the pain and remain open to the next thing that comes up. Keep watching each experience, whatever it is, labeling it, and letting it pass in order to be open to what comes next.

Let it all happen as you watch: thoughts...sensations...feelings. It's all just weather while you are the sky. Just passing weather...to watch...and label... and let go.

How do you feel after completing the mindfulness exercise? Was it challenging for you? If so, that's expected. The struggle is normal, and you'll never be perfect at it. Try to make it a regular practice. In addition, you need to allow yourself the space to honor your grief, to acknowledge your struggle and your suffering. It's a normal part of life. The more you try to push it away, the more you will struggle.

In chapter 8 we discussed walking as a mindfulness activity. And, as you just read in the previous chapter, going for a walk is an act of self-compassion. Walking outside provides so many benefits to increase well-being. Walking is a way to connect with your body, keeping you more present in your experience. Combining walking with green and blue space (plant and water environments) increases the benefits to mood and mental health. There is an abundance of research that confirms that nature plays a causal role in improving mood in the short term. Even sitting or lying in a park or under a tree in your yard can positively affect mood and cognitive functioning, including working memory, and it's proven to decrease anxiety (Bratman et al. 2019).

If you live in an area with easy and open access to nature, take advantage of your fortunate circumstances. If you live in a city, it might not be as easy for you, but you can take advantage of parks, private gardens that provide access during specific hours, and green spaces that are often located throughout urban areas. Aquatic and marine environments might be an option for you.

Sometimes experiencing the emotional pain associated with loss can make you want to withdraw and isolate yourself in your home. This is even easier to do if you work remotely. Resist this urge. Get outside knowing that the experience of moving your body in nature will make you feel better.

Adopting a Gratitude Practice

When you're experiencing the emotions associated with loss, it's easy to lose sight of what's good in your life. Our minds are pre-wired with a negativity bias because we are on high alert for potential threats to our survival, so it takes more effort to notice and acknowledge the positive aspects of our lives. Adopting a daily gratitude practice sets an intention to focus for a dedicated period of time on some of the things that you are grateful for in your life. Gratitude is a proven antidote to negativity.

Benefits of practicing gratitude include the positive impacts on mood, such as increased happiness and positive attitude, as well as physical well-being: better health, improved sleep, less fatigue and burnout, and lower levels of inflammation. And a positive outlook on life can lead to greater resiliency; more satisfaction; reduced focus on materialistic aspects; and the development of patience, humility, and wisdom. In other words, gratitude journaling offers a big reward—increasing your optimism during a time that you might be feeling sad and hopeless (Miller 2019).

Gratitude

Choose a time that works best for you for a regular, ongoing gratitude practice. Using your journal, write down three things that you are grateful for. You might find this difficult at first. Starting small will make it easier to adopt this practice. And you might find it best to do it at the end of the day. Here's an example:

I'm grateful for:

1. *The cup of French roast coffee that I drank this morning.*
2. *The person who held the door open for me at my office building.*
3. *The dog who came up to me when I was sitting on a bench in the park.*

As you may have already surmised, this practice will help you bring attention to the things that usually go unnoticed or that aren't remembered, especially during the times you're feeling sad or struggling. Even during times of hopelessness, there are experiences we can bring attention to that will remind us that life is not all bad. It will help to pull you out of the black-and-white thinking (*Everything is bad*) that often hijacks our minds. This is also a practice that will help you meet the goal of consistent journaling (Korb 2015).

Forgiveness

If you're reading this when you're in the anger stage of grief, it's unlikely that you are in a forgiving mood. But you won't be stuck in this stage forever, and you will need as many helpful tools as possible to process your loss. Holding on to the negative feelings takes a toll on our mental and physical well-being. What if I told you that studies show that forgiving someone who has treated you badly, whether they deserve it or not, has positive benefits—it reduces pain, anxiety, depression, stress, and blood pressure? Plus, you sleep better (Johns Hopkins Medicine n.d.).

You don't need to contact the person to tell them that you forgive them. You can forgive them by writing a letter in your journal that you don't mail. Earlier you practiced self-compassion by accessing your wounded child. Do you think you can imagine the person who wronged you as a wounded child to develop compassion for them? Try it. Forgive the child in the person who hurt you. Do it for yourself.

Moving Forward

You are on a new path that will lead you toward the healthy relationships that you deserve. But it doesn't mean that the emotions associated with grief and loss will go away. They will come and go like waves. Accept them. Observe them without judgment. Your past wasn't perfect, but you're here now. You've survived, and you're on a path to thrive.

CHAPTER 10

The New Dating Game

We thought the best approach to this chapter was for me (Dr. Michelle Skeen) to take you through a few of the most common scenarios that have been presented to me by readers of *Love Me, Don't Leave Me*, my previous book, as well as clients in my therapy and coaching practice. I've also heard these same stories from friends, friends of friends, the person next to me on the airplane, my dental hygienist—the list goes on. Suffice it to say, if any of these scenarios resonate with you, you are not alone.

Once you've broken free of a trauma bond or ended a toxic relationship, you might feel confident that you "learned your lesson" and you'll never fall into that trap again. In hindsight, you'll have clarity about the red flags that you ignored and that you wouldn't ignore as your current self (*The old me didn't know any better*). But the traps are still out there, and what isn't a trap may look like a trap in your current hypervigilant state.

Below are some common dating traps.

Coming in Hot

You meet someone on a dating app. You had easy exchanges over text. You got each other's humor. They were complimentary of you—you're funny, you're hot, you're smart. Unfortunately, they weren't going to be able to meet up with you in person for a few weeks because they had to travel on business or they were going on a scuba diving trip with their best friend. It was too bad because it was obvious that the two of you were going to hit it off in person. Their texting might be limited while they're gone, but they are excited to show you pictures from the trip when they get back and you two could finally get together in person, when undoubtedly the sparks would fly. So, you spend the two weeks they are gone fantasizing about this person, whom you had communicated with only through an app.

During those two weeks, you get a few messages but nothing significant, and they certainly aren't like the ones you received before they left on the trip. But, you think, *Whatever, we'll catch up when we get together. They're busy. I'm busy too, although I would definitely make time for them. Hmmm,* you think to yourself or say out loud to a friend, *I thought they said they were back on the thirteenth and we'd do something on the sixteenth, but it's already the fifteenth. Maybe I should just send them a text. I'm sure it's been busy getting back to the office after being out for two weeks.* So you text. Quick response back. That's a good sign. However, the content is disappointing. "Hey there, thanks for reaching out. I've been so slammed with work I completely forgot that we made plans to get together tomorrow night. I'll get back to you to make a new plan. Thanks."

So what happened, and why are you, as the person who received that text, so disappointed? It's so easy to get caught up in the fantasy of a person and a relationship with them based solely on a fun text exchange. We stop paying attention to the reality of the situation. You haven't met this person. In fact, it is surprising how many of these connections that seem so promising over text end before an in-person meeting. Some people appreciate the ease with which they can get a dopamine hit just by going on a dating app and matching with someone. Maybe they just want to know that others still find them attractive enough to swipe right. They might want nothing more than that. You won't know what they want without asking questions. So how do you steer clear of this dating trap?

First, think about what you want. If you want a relationship in real life, then you need to set some expectations for yourself about what you'll allow regarding texting. You could establish, for example, that after six positive text exchanges on six different days, you want to talk—enough exchanges that you've established that you want to talk. So, stage two could be a phone call unless you're ready to meet in person. You need the information that only an in-person meeting can provide. If they're reluctant to meet then, you have some important information. You might not have the same goals. Don't allow yourself to get strung along over text.

Undeniable Chemistry

Physical attraction and the associated chemistry can often blind us to the other aspects that are misaligned. But we've all seen the rom-coms where the two people from different backgrounds, with opposite life-styles, and with no common hobbies overcome all the obstacles to be together because their attraction to each other is the only thing that matters. The rest will come with time. We love those movies. They give us hope. The point is, it's easy to lose sight of our values, interests, and goals when we are strongly attracted to someone. It's not unlike the "intensity" we covered in chapter 5.

Our desire to be with this person can also, consciously or unconsciously, prevent us from asking questions, because we don't want to know the answers. It's not uncommon for me to hear from someone that they want to be in a long-term monogamous relationship, but they don't know what the other person wants. What did they say on their profile about what they're looking for? "I don't know." Okay, that's not the same as something casual, but it could be, and it might be closer to that than a long-term relationship. If this is important to you, you should ask. By not asking the question, you've already placed your needs and desires beneath the needs and desires of this person, who is one step away from a complete stranger. Honor yourself and your values and ask the question. Pull off the bandage. And, if it's not the answer that matches yours, then move on.

Excuses…Excuses

If you grew up in a family with a caregiver who struggled with addiction or mental health, it's likely that you experienced inconsistent or erratic behavior that was followed by an apology, a promise, or changed behavior—until it happened again. Or maybe you grew up in a family where communication was unhealthy or inconsistent. You might have been ignored or iced-out when your caregiver was upset with you. You may not have understood what you did wrong, and you weren't provided a chance for repair. You just had to wait until they got over it and decided to talk to you again. These types of early relationship experiences can set you up for a pattern of accepting behavior that you otherwise wouldn't.

Bringing awareness to your values as they relate to your relationships will help you avoid getting trapped in a cycle that won't get you closer to the healthy relationship you deserve. It's essential that you express what's important to you early on. "I really value good communication. I function best with consistency." Are you feeling anxious just thinking about expressing that need to someone you've just met? That's normal. It can feel uncomfortable to ask for what is reasonable and what you need. But it doesn't get any easier down the line. Do you want to tolerate two months of inconsistent communication and treatment before you say anything? The other person is always going to have an excuse: "I'm traveling for work." "I've been in back-to-back meetings." "I was exhausted after work." "I just needed some downtime." "I have friends visiting." It doesn't matter what they say. The reality is that they don't care about meeting your needs, or they aren't capable. It's better to find out early on so you can move on. Don't let other people's excuses become obstacles to your happiness.

Reality vs. Fantasy

Staying grounded in reality is difficult when it comes to love—specifically intimate relationships. It's easy to get swept away and ignore the truth because sometimes it can be a buzzkill.

Keep a calendar just for recording the experiences of your new relationship. It's not unusual for a client to tell me that they've been seeing so-and-so for two months, and when I suggest we look at a calendar or I look back at my notes, it's been three weeks. "Wow, it seems longer, like I've known them for longer." That can be a great feeling. But time also increases expectations. So, the reality of the amount of time you've known each other might be out of whack with where your expectations have gone. "I feel like it's time to talk about being exclusive." Again, not a problem to have a conversation about being exclusive, but how well do you know this person? So, keep track of the passage of time.

Another reason for the calendar is to keep track of your times together. Knowing each other for three months sounds like a reasonable amount of time to get to know more about someone, but if you've only had three dates in three months, then the amount of time that has passed can't really be used as a measure for how well you know this person or how well they know you. You want to make informed decisions about your relationships. And, if you've only had a few dates over several months, then you'll want to examine the reasons why you aren't spending more time together. Are they unavailable? Too busy? If so, look at these factors next to your values. If you care about time spent with your partner, then this might be the wrong person for you if you're seeing signs that they wouldn't be able to prioritize you if you were in a relationship.

We've encouraged journaling throughout the book. We want to add emphasis on the importance of journaling during the early stages of dating. Here are some of the benefits:

- It helps reduce your anxiety, which can increase during the uncertainty and ambiguity that is inherent in the dating experience.

- It helps break the cycle of obsessive thinking, which is also normal during this period of the unknown.

- It improves awareness and perception of events. This connects to the suggestion of keeping a calendar: it's important to stay clear about what is happening versus the fantasy of what you want to happen.

- It helps regulate emotions and improve overall mood. This is also a great antidote to the roller coaster of emotions that accompanies the dating experience.

When you're dating, bring renewed awareness to the toxic types and toxic behaviors that you identified in chapter 4. It's so easy to get caught up in the newness of a connection that you are temporarily blinded to behaviors that are toxic. Again, recording everything in your journal brings your experience back to reality. And, if you have a trusted friend, ask them if they will help you stay accountable to yourself. After all, this is all about you breaking long-standing patterns that involve relationship trauma bonds, toxic relationships, or toxic people. Use mindfulness to stay present so that you can evaluate your *now* experience through a clear lens, not one that's distorted by your core beliefs.

After reading through the traps that are inherent in the dating world, do you have more awareness of some of the types of people and situations that make you feel vulnerable? Would you like to bring more awareness to those people and situations in an effort to avoid the traps and respond to the triggers with a valued action?

Triggering-Person Action Plan

Respond to the prompts for each type of person that triggers you (McKay et al. 2013). Start with the one who is most triggering.

Triggering person: (Describe the type of person, or if it's a specific person, write their name.)

1. What is the core belief that is triggered for you?

2. What situations trigger this core belief?

3. What specific thoughts come up when this core belief gets triggered?

4. What sensations do you experience when this core belief gets triggered?

5. What feelings come up when this core belief gets triggered?

6. What coping behavior do you engage in when this core belief gets triggered?

7. What are your specific values in this relationship? What kind of person do you want to be in this relationship, regardless of the outcome?

8. What value-driven action can you take in response to the triggering behavior?

Did this exercise help you bring awareness to how easy it is to fall into old patterns of behavior that will take you further away from your identified values? It's much easier to respond in alignment with your values when you create an action plan.

Let's look at how Prema filled out her Triggering-Person Action Plan.

Triggering person: *Someone who doesn't communicate consistently.*

1. What is the core belief that is triggered for you? *Abandonment and emotional deprivation.*

2. What situations trigger this core belief? *When the person I'm dating goes for days without communicating with me or doesn't respond in a timely manner to my communications.*

3. What specific thoughts come up when this core belief gets triggered? *Why is it so hard to take a minute out of your day to send a text or make a quick call? Why don't they want to talk to me? What's wrong with me? Why does this always happen?*

4. What sensations do you experience when this core belief gets triggered? *I feel an emptiness in the pit of my stomach; I feel anxious; I can't concentrate.*

5. What feelings come up when this core belief gets triggered? *I feel unlovable and unimportant.*

6. What coping behavior do you engage in when this core belief gets triggered? *I might call or text them in a way that makes me come across as pathetic.*

7. What are your specific values in this relationship? *Honesty, communication, boundary setting.* What kind of person do you want to be in this relationship, regardless of the outcome? *I want to put me first. I want to demonstrate that I deserve to be valued and respected.*

8. What value-driven action can you take in response to the triggering behavior? *I tell them that, while I hear all of their reasons for why they haven't been in touch with me, I need consistent communication in a relationship in order to make the connection that I desire and deserve.*

Moving Forward

There might be a part of you that still believes, consciously or unconsciously, that you deserved to be treated the way that you were treated in your formative years and in your past and current relationships. You didn't deserve it! We hope that the words on these pages are getting you closer to believing that you deserve healthy love and acceptance. Hopefully, with a better understanding of what happened to you, you can love yourself. When you can love yourself, you will be better equipped to select others who are capable of loving you in the way you deserve to be loved. And you will recognize the behaviors of others that don't reflect the love you deserve.

You are on a new path—a path that will lead you to the healthy loving connections that you long for and deserve. These pages have laid out a map that we've put together throughout this book. There's a lot of information on these pages. You aren't expected to remember everything. It's likely that after completing all the exercises, you will have a good understanding about where potential challenges lie. Bring attention to them. Write them down. Look at them frequently to remind yourself that you can overcome the obstacles. The next chapter will guide you as you put together the map that's specific to your needs. You got this!

CHAPTER 11

A Map for Navigating Your New Path

As you continue to travel your path of breaking free from trauma bonds, ending toxic relationships, and developing healthy attachments, you'll encounter obstacles as well as opportunities for growth. To avoid straying from your path, you'll need to continue to bring awareness to triggering situations and automatic behaviors in response to your triggers. You'll also want to bring awareness to new behaviors that are helpful and promote healthy relationships and attachments. In this final chapter, you'll compile information in your journal that can act as a map, your go-to, when you need to reference the knowledge and skills for moving forward. We'll be revisiting topics and exercises covered in earlier sections of the book to help you develop your map.

Turn to a new section of your journal to begin your map. Let's start at the beginning. In chapter 1, we discussed *attachment style* and *temperament*—two of the building blocks that make you who you are and guide your decision-making in relationships. What were some statements that were relevant for you that impact your relationships or behavior in terms of your attachment style? Which of the traits of your temperament, such as your ability to adapt, are most relevant as you approach dating? Write them down.

In chapter 2, we explored *core beliefs*—beliefs about yourself and your relationship to others that formed, in part, as a result of dysfunctional experiences in childhood. We homed in on the core beliefs linked to relationship trauma bonds, which include abandonment, mistrust and abuse, emotional deprivation, defectiveness, dependence, failure, and subjugation. You took assessments for each of these to determine which play a role in your life. In your map, write down core belief statements that are often relevant when you get triggered or in situations that are triggering to you. Your understanding will help you break free from toxic situations.

In chapter 3, you gained a better understanding of how your attachment style, temperament, and core beliefs interact to influence your behaviors. You identified and began to understand your *coping behaviors*. Now, whenever you experience a relationship event that triggers you, come back to the following exercise, which should be familiar to you.

When you find yourself triggered, this exercise will provide you with the opportunity to examine that triggering relationship event. You will identify the core belief that is being triggered, your automatic coping response, and the outcome—what happens as a result of your behavioral response. At this stage, we can label it a "consequence" because it is getting in the way of moving you closer to a healthy relationship. Understanding how your coping response is keeping you stuck in an RTB is a big step toward change.

Relationship event:

Core belief triggered:

Coping response:

Outcome or consequence:

To see examples of this exercise, refer to chapter 3.

In chapter 4, we outlined various *relationship trauma-bond traps*. You confronted the fact that you're likely unconsciously seeking partners or creating experiences that reinforce the fears that resulted from your trauma. You identified familiar roles and scripts from your childhood that are present in adulthood. To continue building on this knowledge, write down the toxic types you find yourself drawn to in your map. Also, note the toxic behaviors that you commonly experience from someone else as well as the behaviors that you yourself may engage in. Refer to the lists in chapter 4 to complete this exercise.

In chapter 5, we examined the tension between *intensity and intimacy*. Many people who are stuck in RTBs mistake intensity for intimacy. We considered characteristics inherent in an intimate relationship, like safety, patience, respect, and healthy conflict resolution. Again, these may feel aspirational when you're feeling stuck in toxicity. But now you're on the path toward healing. You're preparing to transition from an RTB to a loving and lasting relationship. In your map, list the qualities of an intimate relationship that are most important to you, that make you feel hopeful, that get you excited for your future. Once you've done that, identify people in your life who represent these healthy qualities. And if you can't think of someone in your life, is there a relationship you admire that represents one or more of these qualities? It can be a real or fictional relationship.

In chapter 6, we discussed the importance of *values*. Your values are a guide for how you want to behave, how you want to treat others, how you want to treat yourself, and how you want others to treat you as you attempt to get your needs met in relationships. In your map, write down your most important values as well as the ones that are especially relevant when you're dating or in a new relationship. If there's overlap between those two lists, that's great because it demonstrates that you're primed to apply your key values in your dating life.

In chapter 7, we did a deep dive into *communication* and its role in relationships. We discussed unhealthy communication patterns, including blocks to listening. In your map, write down the blocks that tend to get in the way of you having healthy communication. Communication blocks include mind reading, filtering, placating, sparring, judging, and comparing. This way, you can bring awareness to your most common pitfalls that get in the way of effective communication. If you struggle with setting boundaries, make a note about boundaries that are important to you and strategies you find useful to maintain them, especially when you feel triggered or tested.

In chapter 8, we explored *mindfulness* as a tool to break unhelpful patterns by bringing awareness to your moment-by-moment experience. When you're feeling overwhelmed by your emotions as the result of a triggering person or situation, use mindfulness as a pause. Look back to chapter 8 to dive into several mindfulness exercises, like the outdoor walk. Here we'll highlight a daily exercise that you can practice whenever you need to feel grounded, even if you only have a few minutes. You can copy it down on your map.

This mindfulness exercise will take five minutes. Set a timer. Sit comfortably in a chair, or if it's easier for you, lie down. Close your eyes. Bring your attention to your thoughts. When a thought enters your mind, notice it without judging, criticizing, or trying to change it. You'll notice that the thoughts keep coming like leaves floating down a stream, clouds moving across the sky, or luggage turning on an airport carousel. You might be having the thought that it's difficult to hang onto a thought. Thoughts come and go. You might find yourself slipping into judgments of liking some thoughts or wanting to push away unpleasant thoughts. Just keep bringing your attention back to observing your thoughts without judgment.

Doing this mindfulness exercise on a routine basis, ideally in the morning, will help you detach from your core-belief-related thoughts. Start with five minutes and build up to ten minutes. After you finish your morning mindfulness practice, see if you can take the attention, openness, and acceptance of the experience into your day.

In chapter 9, we talked through how you can *process the loss* of your relationship and accept your *grieving process* without judgment. Identify the stage of grief that you're in—if that is something that's current for you—so you can be aware of what might be operating unconsciously.

Bringing awareness to your feelings of grief and loss is validating, and it helps you bring awareness to harmful thought patterns and behavior.

Chapter 10 highlighted strategies for identifying potential partners as well as tips and tools to guide you through the obstacles inherent in *dating*. Identify the scenarios that resonate with you the most. Write them in your journal so you can refer to them when you're in the early stages of dating to avoid your usual traps and be prepared to respond appropriately to your triggers. It's easy to lose sight of your values when you're distracted by a new person.

Moving Forward

Consider the relationships and experiences that brought you to this book. Through all that you've discovered about yourself, how do you think differently about those relationships and experiences now? What new relationships and experiences do you want to seek out in this next chapter of your life? How will you continue to bring awareness to the toxic types and traps that may come up for you? When you find yourself triggered, it's tempting to stray from your path and lean into how you've behaved and handled situations in the past. With your newfound tools for navigating challenges, you'll try to stay grounded, engaging in healthy behaviors and situations. We know that this new path won't always be easy, but we hope that you see the value in the work you've already put in and feel confident in your ability to keep going.

Acknowledgments

The Path from *Love Me, Don't Leave Me* to *Why Can't I Let You Go?*

Since the publication of *Love Me Don't Leave Me*, I've received countless emails from readers around the world. I knew from these emails as well as from my therapy and coaching practice that everyone with an abandonment core belief shares common experiences when faced with the threat of abandonment—intolerable emotions, negative thoughts, fear-driven behaviors, and relationship challenges. While I addressed relationship triggers and traps in *LMDLM*, I couldn't ignore the need to do a deeper dive into the relationships—specifically relationship trauma bonds and toxic relationships—that have been a common theme with my readers and clients. This book would not have happened without my readers and clients. I am constantly inspired and impressed by your courage, your ability to be vulnerable, and your desire to be in a healthy, loving relationship despite the obstacles you've overcome and still struggle with. Thank you for sharing your stories with me. You are not alone, and you are loved.

The idea for *Why Can't I Let You Go?* started to take shape during a visit Kelly and I made to Matt and Jude McKay's home in the country during the social-distancing days of the COVID-19 pandemic. While the four of us sat outside, I described my idea for this book. Everyone agreed that it was a necessary and natural follow-up to *LMDLM*. Then Matt looked at Kelly and said, "You should write it with her." And here we are. Thank you, Matt, for always being inspiring and supportive. Our shared interests brought us together as professor/mentor and student, and our shared values (and core beliefs) have bonded us as dear friends. Thank you for always believing in me even when I don't believe in myself.

This book would not be what it is without Elizabeth Hollis Hansen, acquisitions manager, and Vicraj Gill, senior editor, at New Harbinger Publications. In fact, this book may never have made it to the finish line without them! Kelly and I are so grateful for your wise counsel, patience, and attention to detail as you guided us through this process. And, a big shout out goes to Gretel Hakanson, who brought a fresh pair of eyes and the extraordinary editing expertise that we needed.

How do I thank my coauthor and daughter, Kelly? This is our third book together. The first, *Communication Skills for Teens*, was started when she was in high school; *Just as You Are* was started when she was in college; and this book was written while she was thriving in her career. Timewise it didn't make sense for her to be involved in such a time-consuming project, but her values (and some pressure from Matt and me) led her to say yes. At times it was stressful, and we leaned on our communication skills, specifically—active listening, clarification, and feedback—to get us through those times. But we also had fun working toward the goal of writing a book designed to alleviate some of the pain inherent in trauma bonds and toxic relationships. Kelly, thank you for being exactly who you are. I couldn't love you more.

Heart hugs,
Michelle

I often laugh when sharing with people in my life that I coauthor self-help books with my mom. It's certainly not your typical mother-daughter bonding activity. But our collaboration speaks to the strength and multi-faceted nature of our relationship as well as our shared passion for serving others. We find it incredibly meaningful to connect with readers around the world about the things we hold most dear in life—love and connection—and those that challenge us most—trauma, grief, and loss. When you're feeling alone, please know that we're here on the other side of the page, sending you compassion and support.

Thanks for navigating this path with us,
Kelly

Additional Resources

Trauma

The Betrayal Bond: Breaking Free of Exploitative Relationships by Patrick J. Carnes

The Body Keeps the Score: Brain, Mind, and Body in the Healing of Trauma by Bessel van der Kolk

Attachment

Attached: The New Science of Adult Attachment and How It Can Help You Find—and Keep—Love by Amir Levine and Rachel S. F. Heller

Love Me, Don't Leave Me: Overcoming Fear of Abandonment and Building Lasting, Loving Relationships by Michelle Skeen

Core Beliefs

Reinventing Your Life: The Breakthrough Program to End Negative Behavior… and Feel Great Again by Jeffrey E. Young and Janet S. Klosko

Coping Behaviors

Fear: Essential Wisdom for Getting Through the Storm by Thich Nhat Hanh

The Interpersonal Problems Workbook: ACT to End Painful Relationship Patterns by Matthew McKay, Patrick Fanning, Avigail Lev, and Michelle Skeen

User's Guide to the Human Mind: Why Our Brains Make Us Unhappy, Anxious, and Neurotic and What We Can Do About It by Shawn T. Smith

Breaking Unhelpful Habits

The Craving Mind: From Cigarettes to Smartphones to Love—Why We Get Hooked and How We Can Break Bad Habits by Judson Brewer

Discipline is Destiny: The Power of Self-Control by Ryan Holiday

Values

Four Thousand Weeks: Time Management for Mortals by Oliver Burkeman

Developing Healthy Communication

The Art of Communicating by Thich Nhat Hanh

Nonviolent Communication: A Language of Life by Marshall B. Rosenberg

Mindfulness

The Daily Stoic: 366 Meditations on Wisdom, Perseverance, and the Art of Living by Ryan Holiday

The Miracle of Mindfulness by Thich Nhat Hanh

Stillness Is the Key by Ryan Holiday

Waking Up: A Guide to Spirituality Without Religion by Sam Harris

Waking Up Meditation App with Sam Harris

Grief and Loss

A Fearless Heart: How the Courage to Be Compassionate Can Transform Our Lives by Thupten Jinpa

The Upward Spiral: Using Neuroscience to Reverse the Course of Depression, One Small Change at a Time by Alex Korb

When Life Hits Hard: How to Transcend Grief, Crisis, and Loss with Acceptance and Commitment Therapy by Russ Harris

Healthy Attachments and Love

Courage Is Calling: Fortune Favors the Brave by Ryan Holiday

Ego Is the Enemy by Ryan Holiday

The Obstacle Is the Way: The Timeless Art of Turning Trials into Triumph by Ryan Holiday

Real Love: The Art of Mindful Connection by Sharon Salzberg

References

Barkley, S. 2022. "What is Repetition Compulsion?" PsychCentral, September 16. https://psychcentral.com/blog/repetition-compulsion -why-do-we-repeat-the-past.

BetterHelp Editorial Team. 2023. "What Can a Temperament Test Tell Me About Myself, and Where Can I Take One?" *BetterHelp*. Updated April 3, 2023. https://www.betterhelp.com/advice /temperament/what-does-a-temperament-test-tell-me-about-myself -and-where-can-i-take-one.

Bidjerano, T. 2011. "Thomas and Chess Classification of Infant." In *Encyclopedia of Child Behavior and Development*, edited by S. Goldstein and J. A. Naglieri. Boston, MA: Springer.

Bratman, G. N., C. B. Anderson, M. G. Berman, B. Cochran, S. de Vries, J. Flanders, et al. 2019. "Nature and Mental Health: An Ecosystem Perspective." *Science Advances* 5(7): eaax0903.

Carnes, P. J. 2019. *The Betrayal Bond: Breaking Free of Exploitive Relationships*. Deerfield Beach, FL: Health Communications.

Cherelus, G. 2023. "'Ghosting,' 'Orbiting,' 'Rizz': A Guide to Modern Dating Terms." *New York Times*, February 11. https://www.nytimes .com/2023/02/11/style/dating-terms-guide-ghosting-rizz.html.

Chess, S., and A. Thomas. 1996. *Temperament: Theory and Practice*. New York: Routledge.

Conrad, M. 2023. "What Is Gaslighting? Meaning and Examples." *Forbes*. Updated May 18, 2023. https://www.forbes.com/health/mind /what-is-gaslighting.

Davis, D. M., and J. A. Hayes. 2011. "What Are the Benefits of Mindfulness? A Practice Review of Psychotherapy-Related Research." *Psychotherapy* 48(2): 198–208.

Harris, R. 2021a. *Trauma-Focused ACT: A Practitioner's Guide to Working with Mind, Body, and Emotion Using Acceptance and Commitment Therapy.* Oakland, CA: Context Press.

———. 2021b. *When Life Hits Hard: How to Transcend Grief, Crisis, and Loss with Acceptance and Commitment Therapy.* Oakland, CA: New Harbinger Publications.

Harvard Health Publishing. 2022. "The Power of Self-Compassion." *Harvard Medical School.* February 2. https://www.health.harvard .edu/healthbeat/the-power-of-self-compassion.

Johns Hopkins Medicine. n.d. "Forgiveness: Your Health Depends on It." *Johns Hopkins.* http://hopkinsmedicine.org/health/wellness-and -prevention/forgiveness-your-health-depends-on-it.

Korb, A. 2015. *The Upward Spiral: Using Neuroscience to Reverse the Course of Depression, One Small Change at a Time.* Oakland, CA: New Harbinger Publications.

McKay, M., M. Davis, and P. Fanning. 2009. *Messages: The Communication Skills Book.* Oakland, CA: New Harbinger Publications.

McKay, M., P. Fanning, A. Lev, and M. Skeen. 2013. *The Interpersonal Problems Workbook: ACT to End Painful Relationship Patterns.* Oakland, CA: New Harbinger Publications.

McKay, M., A. Lev, and M. Skeen. 2012. *Acceptance and Commitment Therapy for Interpersonal Problems: Using Mindfulness, Acceptance, and Schema Awareness to Change Interpersonal Behaviors.* Oakland, CA: New Harbinger Publications.

Miller, K. D. 2019. "14 Benefits of Practicing Gratitude (Incl. Journaling)." *Positive Psychology,* June 18. http://positivepsychology .com/benefits-of-gratitude.

Nhat Hanh, T. 2012. *Fear: Essential Wisdom for Getting Through the Storm*. San Francisco: HarperOne.

———. 2013. *The Art of Communicating*. San Francisco, CA: HarperOne.

Rosenberg, M. B. 2015. *Nonviolent Communication: A Language of Life: Life-Changing Tools for Healthy Relationships*. Encinitas, CA: PuddleDancer Press.

Salzberg, S. 2018. *Real Love: The Art of Mindful Connection*. New York: Flatiron Books.

Simpson, J., W. S. Rholes, and D. Phillips. 1996. "Conflict in Close Relationships: An Attachment Perspective." *Journal of Personality and Social Psychology* 71: 899–914.

Skeen, M. 2014. *Love Me, Don't Leave Me: Overcoming Fear of Abandonment and Building Lasting, Loving Relationships*. Oakland, CA: New Harbinger Publications.

Smith, S. T. 2011. *The User's Guide to the Human Mind: Why Our Brains Make Us Unhappy, Anxious, and Neurotic and What We Can Do About It*. Oakland, CA: New Harbinger Publications.

van der Kolk, B. 2015. *The Body Keeps the Score: Brain, Mind, and Body in the Healing of Trauma*. New York: Penguin.

van Vreeswijk, M., J. Broersen, and G. Schurink. 2014. *Mindfulness and Schema Therapy: A Practical Guide*. Hoboken, NJ: Wiley-Blackwell.

Yang, C., A. Barrós-Loscertales, M. Li, D. Pinazo, V. Borchardt, C. Ávila, and M. Walter. 2019. "Alterations in Brain Structure and Amplitude of Low-frequency After 8 Weeks of Mindfulness Meditation Training in Meditation-Naïve Subjects." *Scientific Reports* 9: 10977.

Young, J. E., and J. S. Klosko. 1994. *Reinventing Your Life: The Breakthrough Program to End Negative Behavior...and Feel Great Again*. New York: Penguin.

Young, J. E., J. S. Klosko, and M. E. Weishaar. 2006. *Schema Therapy: A Practitioner's Guide*. New York: Guilford Press.

Michelle Skeen, PsyD, has a doctorate in clinical psychology. She is author of *Love Me, Don't Leave Me* and six other books. Her passion is coaching individuals in creating and maintaining healthy relationships by bringing awareness to core beliefs and the related patterns of behavior, which often work unconsciously to limit connections with others. Michelle believes that an early introduction and education in core values and healthy communication are essential life skills for success. To that end, Michelle and her daughter, Kelly, coauthored *Just As You Are* and *Communication Skills for Teens*.

Skeen completed her postdoctoral work at the University of California, San Francisco. She codeveloped an empirically validated protocol for the treatment of interpersonal problems that resulted in two books: *Acceptance and Commitment Therapy for Interpersonal Problems* and *The Interpersonal Problems Workbook*. Michelle's books have been translated into thirteen languages, and her work has appeared in more than thirty publications around the world. To find out more, visit her website at www.michelle skeen.com.

Kelly Skeen is a graduate of Georgetown University in Washington, DC, with a degree in American Studies, Education, and Spanish. She is an art museum professional, developing meaningful gallery experiences aimed at enhancing visitor engagement. Skeen is skilled at distilling complex concepts for non-specialist audiences, including museum visitors and self-help readers. She is coauthor of *Just As You Are* and *Communication Skills for Teens* with her mother, Michelle Skeen. To learn more, visit her website at www.kellyskeen.com.

MORE BOOKS from
NEW HARBINGER PUBLICATIONS

**DISARMING
THE NARCISSIST,
THIRD EDITION**

Surviving and Thriving
with the Self-Absorbed

9781684037704 / US $17.95

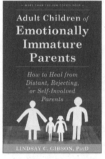

**ADULT CHILDREN
OF EMOTIONALLY
IMMATURE PARENTS**

How to Heal from Distant,
Rejecting, or Self-Involved Parents

978-1626251700 / US $18.95

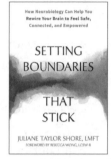

**SETTING BOUNDARIES
THAT STICK**

How Neurobiology Can
Help You Rewire Your Brain
to Feel Safe, Connected,
and Empowered

978-1648481291 / US $18.95

**DISTRESS TOLERANCE
MADE EASY**

Dialectical Behavior Therapy
Skills for Dealing with Intense
Emotions in Difficult Times

978-1648482373 / US $18.95

**THE EMOTIONALLY
EXHAUSTED WOMAN**

Why You're Feeling
Depleted and How to
Get What You Need

978-1648480157 / US $18.95

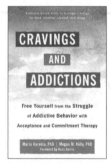

**CRAVINGS AND
ADDICTIONS**

Free Yourself from
the Struggle of Addictive
Behavior with Acceptance
and Commitment Therapy

978-1684038336 / US $17.95

newharbingerpublications
1-800-748-6273 / newharbinger.com

(VISA, MC, AMEX / prices subject to change without notice)
Follow Us 🅾 📘 🐦 ▶️ 📌 in

Don't miss out on new books from New Harbinger.
Subscribe to our email list at **newharbinger.com/subscribe**